Extra Virgin

Extra

an australian companion to olives and

Virgin

olive oil by karen reichelt with michael burr

Wakefield Press

Wakefield Press
Box 2266
Kent Town
South Australia 5071

First published 1997
Reprinted 2000

Edited by Jane Arms
Typography by Liz Nicholson, design BITE, Adelaide
Cover design by Liz Nicholson, design BITE, Adelaide
Cover photograph by Catherine Gasmier
Typeset by Clinton Ellicott, MoBros, Adelaide
Printed and bound in Australia by Hyde Park Press, Adelaide

National Library of Australia
Cataloguing-in-publication entry

Reichelt, Karen
Extra virgin: an Australian companion to olives and olive oil

Bibliography
Includes index
ISBN 1 86254 417 4

1. Olive-Australia. 2. Olive oil-Australia.
3. Olive oil industry-Australia. 4. Cookery (Olive oil).
I. Burr, M. (Michael). II. Title.

634.630994

Promotion of this book has been assisted
by the South Australian Government
through Arts South Australia.

Wakefield Press thanks Wirra Wirra Vineyards
and Arts South Australia for their support.

contents

on the flame

foreword by stefano manfredi

Since the early days of this once British colony, the olive tree has
been scattered throughout. There have always been a few individuals – eccentrics
and visionaries who, having a sense of the potential of this ancient tree,
encouraged the planting of olives in Australia. The problem, until recently,
has been the English tradition of dripping, mutton and overcooked vegetables.
Consequently, oil produced locally was used as a tonic with castor oil, as a
sun-oil or to massage babies' heads. Olive trees were deemed decorative and
stands of them used as windbreaks.

Little did these first pioneers realise that they were planting saplings, not
just of a tree but of an entire culture of food that in time would subvert their own
English way of eating. The olive waited patiently. Even though many groves

were abandoned through lack of interest, the trees took hold and in some places, like in parts of South Australia, they went feral and were regarded as pests. That is until the great post-war migration of people from the countries around the Mediterranean. This migration has successfully spilled the Mediterranean sensibility about the table to much of Australia. Perhaps the greatest cultural influence on Australia has been the food, and at the heart of Mediterranean cooking is olive oil.

When I was a kid in the sixties, Australians thought we wogs ate strange food. We would go into pet shops and buy horse meat to take home and eat! We would go to school with strange, not-square bread filled with chocolate instead of vegemite and we dressed our salads and our vegetables and cooked our meat and fish with strangely pungent olive oil. Back then, Australians looked on this oil as a peculiar product used exclusively by the Italians, Greeks, Spanish and so on.

Over the past generation, however, something quite remarkable has taken place. Olive oil has begun to be revered as an indispensable flavour of modern cooking. It has taken its place in Australia in much the same way as it has done in the Mediterranean. Those Mediterranean migrants have influenced our restaurants to the point where a new generation of chefs has taken olive oil and made it a mandatory ingredient of the Australian pantry. Australians have learnt about these migrant cuisines through restaurants and the restaurant revolution as well as commentary by influential magazines such as *Vogue Entertaining* and *Gourmet Traveller.*

It seems as though, as a nation, we have reached the point where we discuss food as much as sport and olive oil as much as who is going to captain Australia on the next Ashes tour. Karen Reichelt has written a historical perspective of olive oil in this country. She has taken the melting pot of the early settlers, the migrants and the modern culinary revolution and linked it in a historical sense. *Extra Virgin* tells us who and why, as well as how, olive oil came to be so important in a country that has reached its culinary adolescence. It is a history that we need to acknowledge if we are to maintain our progress, particularly when it comes to producing our own great olive oil – a task that is still before us. We need to understand that national pride alone will not make a great olive oil. After all, the great oils of the old world took thousands of years to develop and, in that sense, we are not doing too badly.

the olive in history

'I was born in Australia to Greek and Turkish parents.
My mother used to send us kids to the old Adelaide gaol
and to the parklands near North Terrace to collect olives
for pickling.' **Zeffie Kathreptis**

In the years following the second world war, Australia was peacefully invaded and benignly conquered by Mediterranean cuisine. Even the most timid eaters found themselves venturing on modest culinary journeys, and one of their most entrancing and seductive discoveries was olive oil. For some, olive oil was a new experience.

But even those who had known about olive oil for years had never suspected it might be something a good deal more wondrous than merely a palliative for constipation or a cleaning agent for the dog's ears. As the truth about this ancient fruit and its amazing oil gradually dawned on Australians, demand for it grew and a pleasant addiction began. From using olives stuffed with pimento exclusively at cocktail parties – the style of the 1960s – Australians have become, like all users of olive oil down the centuries, passionate about it. That passion is reflected in our markets and delicatessens, which spill over with olives and olive oil – in tins and fancy bottles, marinated, transformed into olive breads and tapenades and in innumerable other guises, testifying to its stunning versatility.

While Australia's chefs – amateur and professional – vary in their choice of favourites among the ever-widening range of olive oils available, they all agree on one thing: olive oil is wonderful. Olives and olive oil are now found on the most casual and the most elegant tables. Good olive oil can be enjoyed with just a piece of fresh bread or it can play a subtle and critical role in the most complex dishes. Along this spectrum from utter simplicity to the highest sophistication, the culinary possibilities are endless.

Bouyed by the rise and rise of the olive and its oil, farmers all over the country are replacing crops with olive groves and investors are sinking money into this liquid gold. To adapt the feverish language of advertising, olive oil is not the flavour of the month, it's the flavour of the decade. It is trendy and healthy at the same time; nature's perfect food.

The story of olive oil in Australia is mostly the story of enthusiasts and aficionados working in isolation and against the odds. The colonial culinary inheritance from Britain did not include a love of olive oil. Its European provenance and associations put olive oil from the start beyond the pale for Anglophile colonists intent on sheep and cattle farming. The roast beef of old England, the leg of lamb on Sundays, and vegetables tortured beyond taste in boiling water were central to Australian cuisine until the European immigrant influx of the 1950s and 1960s. But in enclaves and pockets all over the country, the early groundwork for an eventual olive oil culture was carried out by eccentrics, enthusiasts and visionaries throughout the nineteenth century.

So it is not as surprising as it might seem that Greek and Italian migrants arriving in Australia after the war discovered with delight century-old olive trees surrounding many of the capital cities and gracing their hills. The only puzzle they found in all this was the lack of enthusiasm of their Australian neighbours.

Olive harvesting has now become an Australian winter pastime. Families scour the hills and country roads for wild olives, taking home hessian bags full of them for preserving.

Though the Australian industry is still young, some Australian olive oils are gaining burgeoning reputations. The producers vary in their approach, some believing the best oils are produced by traditional methods with technology kept to a minimum, others preferring the scientific, technological approach.

But however we go about it, whether fossicking through the hills with our families or participating in the growing agricultural olive revolution, we are now worshipping the olive and its oil with almost as much fervour as our ancient ancestors. In this respect at least, our two hundred year white history reaches back gratefully to the distant past and the sacred olive.

the olive's journey

Australians have developed a consuming passion for olive oil. Some say the cafe society that developed in the eighties is responsible. It was then that Australians were served oil with bread instead of butter and took to such delicacies as bruschetta, olive bread, oil-based pasta sauces, and gourmet pizzas with gusto. Olive oil had entered mainstream dining.

The demand for olive oil in Australia has risen by more than 300 per cent over the past decade to in excess of 17,000 tonnes. All but 1 per cent is imported. At the same time consumption of table olives has risen by more than 200 per cent to over 8700 tonnes each year with more than three-quarters being imported at a cost of more than $A20 million. We just can't seem to get enough. Top Australian olive oil producers sell all their supplies well before the next year's harvest, and markets and delicatessens are always brimming with plump, luscious olives ready to grace an elaborate or humble table.

Hobby farmers and professional growers all over the country are investing in olive plantations in an olive planting frenzy like the one that occurred last century. In the 1870s South Australian olive production was even seen to be a more viable enterprise than wine production. But it has been a history of boom and bust. Dreams have been shattered and fortunes have been lost.

The olive's delights were not discovered by someone picking and eating the fruit off a tree. Olives are inedible in their natural state and must be treated with water or diluted acid to remove their bitter glycosides.

It had been claimed that Captain John Macarthur first introduced the olive to Australia in the nineteenth century. But that honour actually belongs to a humble market gardener called George Suttor, a protegé of Sir Joseph Banks. According to the *Historical Record of New South Wales*, volume 17, part 2, Suttor landed in Sydney on 28 December 1800 with a collection of plants including a single olive tree. It was said to have

arrived in a healthy condition, and it probably survived under Suttor's attention. There is no definite record of the plant's destination, but it is safe to assume that it was planted in the Sydney Botanic Gardens.

Suttor returned to England in 1810 but came back to Sydney two years later. The Sydney *Gazette* reported on Suttor's activities on 23 May 1812: 'Among some valuable plants introduced to the Colony by Mr Suttor, who returned in the *Mary*, are several plants of the date palm and olive in a healthy state. These plants are native of the Grecian Isles and most parts of Italy, where they are much cultivated, and furnish a great part of food for the inhabitants. From the olives of these countries the best sweet oil is produced, and as a plant flourishes in climates very similar to ours, we have reason to hope it will thrive to perfection here.'

These olives were probably planted at Suttor's private property at Parramatta. A writer in the *Agricultural Gazette of New South Wales* in 1917 said that Suttor was not an assertive man, as a market gardener was low in the social order and it was not in his nature to assert his claim as Australia's father of the olive.

Commissioner Bigge was under the mistaken impression that Macarthur was the first to introduce the olive tree to Australia. In his report on the state of agriculture and trade in the Colony of New South Wales in 1823, he wrote: 'The olive tree has been introduced into the colony by Mr J. Macarthur, and has already manifested indications of early assimilation to the climate. Its growth and progress have exceeded those of the olive tree in the south of Europe. With the view to accelerate the production of olive oil in the Colony, I should recommend that plants should be sent from England by every convenient opportunity in the convict ships, and that these should, in the first instance, be consigned to

BAKED GOAT'S CHEESE AND TOMATO ON BRUSCHETTA

Cut goat's cheese and tomato in 1 cm thick slices, brush well with olive oil and roll in dried bread crumbs. Roast in a 160°C oven for 10 minutes. Brush thick slices of bread with garlic-flavoured olive oil and toast until golden. Serve bruschetta topped with tomato slices and cheese.

PIZZA

Spread a pizza base with tomato paste and drizzle with olive oil. Top with steamed baby spinach, chopped goat's cheese, sliced Roma tomatoes and small black olives. Drizzle with more olive oil and bake in a 220°C oven for about 10 minutes or until the cheese is melted and the base is crisp.

the care and management of the colonial botanist, and afterwards be distributed amongst the respectable settlers who apply for them.'

After the downfall of Napoleon, John Macarthur and two of his sons had travelled through France and Switzerland to study the cultivation of the olive and the vine, and Macarthur did bring olives to New South Wales in 1817 – well after George Suttor. But Macarthur was certainly the first resident to apply his knowledge in Australian conditions.

The cultivation of the olive was a favourite theme of contemporary newspapers. The Sydney *Gazette* and the *Monitor* did not miss any opportunity to have a humorous jibe at each other. Discussing suitable soils for the cultivation of the olive, the editor of the *Gazette* of 3 March 1829 wrote that the *Monitor* editor had betrayed his ignorance on the subject, saying, 'If he would only step into the Government Gardens his scepticism would blush before the triple demonstration of sight, touch and taste.'

The *Town and Country Journal* reported on 11 June 1898 on the fate of olive trees planted some years before from cuttings from Sir Samuel Davenport. One of the planters was Mr William Tomlins, an enterprising dairy farmer on the south coast and one of the presidents of the Berry Agricultural Society. 'The situation of his farm is a bold mountain ridge, and on the side of this ridge the olive truncheons were planted some ten years ago, and they have now been multiplied into over fifty plants. Some of the older trees are now producing annually large quantities of fruit, and they are in healthy and thriving condition, although the situation is exposed and the soil not best for fruit-growing. Mr Tomlins has not made much use of the fruit yet. The fowls he says are very fond of it, and he thinks olive-growing would pay for that purpose alone, as it is good egg-producing food.' Despite efforts by several enthusiastic supporters inspired by Sir Samuel Davenport, the New South Wales industry did not much expand.

In 1829, in Perth, Governor Stirling planted an olive tree at Government House. Years later it was considered good luck to run around the majestic tree three times, which was not easy, because the tree grew on a steep slope. On the way to the races dapper young men would leave their horse and carriage in the street, slip into the gardens and sneak up to the tree to give it the quick run around.

Conservative plantings continued in Western Australia. The Perth *Inquirer* reported in 1843 that two good samples of olive oil had been produced in Western Australia. One was cold drawn, the other was extracted by heat. Both were manufactured by Mr Jones of Woodbridge by a process of his own invention. He had planted the trees seven years earlier when they had been slips two feet long and half an inch in diameter. They had started bearing within four years and at the time of the report were twenty-five feet high.

Despite Suttor and Macarthur, many colonists were tireless in laying claim to some credit for the birth of the Australian olive industry. A few years after the Perth *Inquirer*'s revelation, the *Journal of the Royal Australian Historical Society* recorded that Thomas Livingston Mitchell, soon after his return to England in 1847, 'Gave to the Society of Arts two bottles of olive oil, the first samples ever produced, I believe, in Australia. The oil was made by Mr Kid, superintendent of the Botanic Gardens at Sydney, from olives grown there, and seemed very clear and good.' Mitchell was also reported to have proposed that, 'The civilised Aborigines should be taught the cultivation of the vine and the olive.'

In 1846, Bishop Salvado and the Benedictine monks of New Norcia in

In Homer's time, nine centuries before Christ, frequent mention was made of the olive. On the slopes of the Mount of Olives, to the east of Jerusalem, was the plantation of Gethsemane, which means 'olive press'.

Western Australia planted 150 olive trees. They established the grove north-east of the monastery across the Moore River and planted avenues of olives along the roads. Lord Abbott Torres was awarded the silver medal at the Franco-British Exhibition in 1908 for his exhibition of olive oil produced at the monastery.

While New South Wales and Western Australia were dabbling in olive production, the industry really started in earnest in South Australia. The climate and soil proved perfect for this Mediterranean crop. On his arrival in South Australia in 1836, the colony's foundation year, Governor Hindmarsh brought with him an olive tree. This tree was planted by Mr George Stevenson in his North Adelaide garden. The Adelaide *Observer* followed the fate of this pioneer plant: 'The slip brought out seven years ago has borne fruit. The tree is an exceedingly handsome one, and measures nine feet in height, and seven in diameter. The olive is cultivated with far less trouble and expense than the vine, and will grow anywhere; and its yield as valuable an article of export. We hope to see its growth and cultivation encouraged in South Australia.'

The next recorded olive imports were in 1844. The South Australian Company brought five of the best oil-producing varieties from Marseilles. They were Bouquetier, Silouen, Blanquette, Redonaou and Verdale.

In June 1875, in the *South Australian Register*, it was reported: 'The trees were propagated in many of the early gardens, particularly in the neighbourhood of Adelaide. Their foliage interspersed as it is at this time of year with the clustering drooping fruit renders them picturesque objects, and their berries have for a long time been utilised more or less by families in the shape of "picholines" pickled olives, or even in the making of small quantities of oil, which is the most excellent quality, honourable mention

The Greeks regarded the olive with reverence, and olive groves were sacred ground which only virgins and chaste men could cultivate. In sixth century Athens, anyone caught cutting down an olive tree was executed.

having been obtained in the London Exhibition of 1851 ...The Adelaide Corporation, having due appreciation of the value of the olive, have had about 30,000 trees planted on the Park Lands surrounding the city. Some 5000 or 6000 of these adjacent to the Gaol have been bearing for the last few years.'

William Boothby, Sheriff and Electoral Returning Officer of South Australia, conducted a personal demonstration of the value of the Australian olive industry. After planting trees for five or six years on the enclosures around the gaol, he began, with half a ton of fruit, to extract oil in 1870, so beginning his own industry, which he ran from the gaol. The produce was of such a high quality that it was readily bought at eleven shillings a gallon. The following year William Booth by combined the produce of Captain Simpson's Glen Osmond olive yard with that of the Adelaide Corporation plantation and obtained a considerable quantity of oil.

The matter then began to attract attention. Some people were jealous of his operations and he was prohibited from pressing fruit for individual people. The amount received in 1874 for the oil obtained from gaol plantations was sixty-one pounds. It was handed over to the sheriff to buy equipment to develop the industry.

In 1876-77 William Boothby, as Macarthur and his sons had done earlier, made an extensive tour of the olive-growing countries of Europe to learn all he could about all aspects of the industry. On returning he wrote a comprehensive treatise on the subject, entitled *The Olive, its Culture and Products in the South of France and Italy*, which was published by the Government Printing Office in Adelaide. He imported 500 cuttings of the variety Frontoiana from Lucca, in Italy, which were planted in the

Olives appear in folklore throughout the Mediterranean. They were said to ward off all kinds of evils from witches to over-active libidos.

Adelaide Botanic Gardens, but there is no record of what became of them.

Samuel Davenport was yet another genuine pioneer of the Australian olive industry and did everything he could to get it established on an extensive scale. It was his dream to create a new Corfu between Adelaide and Kapunda. Davenport was so enthusiastic about the fledgling olive industry that he wrote in the *South Australian Register* in 1875: 'The golden grain of our fine-skinned wheat, the golden fleece of our Merino sheep, also climatically confirm our qualifications for the production of golden olive oil. Let us declare that, wheat, oil, wine, fine wool and silk are the chief natural products of this part of Australia, and that we will vigorously promote their cultivation ... Another, and not the least, recommendation of the olive is that after once coming into bearing it is increasing every year in its productiveness, and lives to such an age that once planted in a suitable situation, which may be found almost all over this colony, it is practically planted forever, becoming a source of wealth to future generations.'

Samuel Davenport gave advice to anyone showing an interest in olives, and gave away cuttings for grafting from his own collection of imported varieties. He erected a pressing plant on his Beaumont property where he produced and marketed excellent olive oil. He also planted an experimental block of olives at Palmer, thirty-three miles east of Adelaide. In 1883 he imported the varieties Sevilano, Temprano, and Loyhayne from Gibraltar, and later he introduced eight varieties from the South of France, of which only the Picholine survived.

Chief Justice Sir Richard Hanson held a banquet in 1876 to acknowledge Samuel Davenport's achievements. By then Davenport had been the president of the Royal Agricultural and Horticultural Society for seven years, and president of the Chamber of Manufactures for twenty years. He had also represented South Australia at the London Exhibition in 1851 and the Philadelphia Exhibition in 1875.

In the proceedings of the banquet, it was recorded: 'No person in the colony has given so much of his time to the suggestion of various branches of industry that might be made available here, or devoted so much time to showing practically and theoretically in what manner they might be turned to account ... It would be difficult to mention any one branch of industry which had not been the object of careful investigation on the part of Mr Davenport.'

Davenport was made a Knight Bachelor in 1884. He went on to represent South Australia at the 1886 London Exhibition and was awarded the KCMG in the same year. He was executive commissioner for South Australia at the Adelaide Jubilee Exhibition in 1887.

The first large-scale attempt to establish olive culture on a commercial basis in Australia was in 1873, when Sydney Clark and William Mair formed the Stonyfell Olive Company at Magill in Adelaide. The first three acres were planted in 1874, and planting was continued until 1882, by which time 100 acres were under cultivation. Clark and Mair obtained scions for grafting from Sir Samuel Davenport. In 1901, the Stonyfell Company employed eighty-six workers.

In 1887, under the South Australian Crown Lands Amendment Act, special twenty-one-year leases, with the right to buy, were granted at a low annual rental or purchase price to encourage olive tree and fruit growing. Some olive trees were planted at this time, notably near Bordertown in the east and Lake Roy, thirty miles to the south-west of Adelaide.

According to the *Koran*, Allah is the light of the heavens and of the earth, a niche wherein a lamp is found, a glass twinkling like a star. It is lit by the sacred olive tree, which has an oil so clear it would give light even if no spark were put to it.

'If I could paint and had the necessary time, I should devote myself for a few years to making pictures only of olive trees.'

Aldous Huxley

Around 1890, the Chaffey brothers, who had initiated the irrigation developments along the Murray River, brought olives to the Riverina. They selected over 100 acres as orchard and nursery land and planted 30,000 vines, oranges and lemons, and fifteen acres of olive trees. Ernestine Hill wrote in 1937 that, 'The trees brought a misty grey-green glory that is one of the outstanding beauties of Renmark today.'

Any existing local demand for olive oil decreased during the depression of the late 1890s. Interest in the development of the olive industry flagged. The British were not noted for their consumption of, or interest in, olives. As well, a plentiful supply of animal fats in Australia, particularly butter, reduced demand for the oil product. The difficulty in acquiring a taste for the olive, which must be processed in exactly the right manner to be palatable, also hindered Australians' acceptance of the fruit. The oil that was produced was used mainly as a sun-oil and for the treatment of cradle cap in babies. In any case, Mediterranean countries had been producing olive oil for centuries and could produce quality oil at a fraction of the cost of the Australian product.

Oil produced at the Adelaide Gaol had to be stockpiled, and in 1897 fifty cases of it were sent to Britain in the hope that it would fetch a better price there. The oil failed to sell at all and was eventually given away to charities. Despite the lack of interest, a few small commercial plantings of oil-producing olives were established around Adelaide and Renmark in South Australia, often as roadside windbreaks. Other plantings were scattered through Victoria and New South Wales. Several small extracting plants were built in these areas.

W.J. Allen wrote in the 1900 *Agricultural Gazette of New South Wales* that olive trees were growing to perfection and fruiting at

In Algeria, there was an ancient olive tree into which the ill drove nails to cure their ailments. In Morocco, a curse would fall on those who entered someone's house carrying olive oil and left without giving some away.

Wentworth and Bourke, two of New South Wales's warmest districts, and that olives were growing well at Moree, Hay, Corowa and Wagga but had not been a success at Wollongbar on the Richmond River. He reported that olives that had been grown under irrigation in Mildura, Victoria, were coming to the front with some good oils. The Dookie Agricultural college near Shepparton in the Goulburn Valley was producing fine oil which was highly acclaimed when tested. He remarked that New South Wales seemed to be behind its sister colonies in this enterprise, and that little, if anything, had been done in the way of either cultivation or oil production. He ascribed this to the state's not having opened any tracts of land in the drier districts that would be suitable for the culture of the olive. He concluded: 'The olive tree is worthy of consideration as one which will yield a profitable return to those who will plant and give it proper attention.'

At the Wagga Experimental Farm in New South Wales, an olive variety collection was established in 1895 by the New South Wales Department of Agriculture. This was later added to, resulting in an extensive collection of both oil and pickling varieties.

In an attempt to resurrect the industry, the South Australian Department of Agriculture established the Blackwood Experimental Orchard in 1908, where they planted twenty-seven olive varieties. In 1914 the department imported three pickling varieties from Spain, and eight other varieties were imported from Roeding, California. Among them was the Mission, which had been taken to America in the sixteenth century by Spanish Jesuit missionaries. The department's 1914 annual report gives a total of thirty-five varieties growing at the orchard.

Professor Arthur J. Perkins, the Director of Agriculture, wrote a bulletin in 1917 on the scope for extension of olive groves in South

Olive oil has been used to bestow irrevocable kinship, to consecrate priests, churches and holy objects, to light sanctuary lamps, and to signify sacramental grace and strength.

Australia. He recommended extended planting of olives, especially as windbreaks on Mallee country farms. As a practical demonstration he planted shelter belts of olives around an experimental farm at Minnipa, on the Eyre Peninsula near Streaky Bay.

In 1920, as a result of Perkins's support of olive culture, the South Australian government approved an annual bonus of ten shillings an acre for ten years for anyone who planted olive trees and tended them in compliance with regulations set by the Department of Agriculture.

Queensland had a brief history of olive production. The first plantings were in 1877. Lewis Adolphus Bernays wrote extensively on the subject in his paper 'Cultural Industries for Queensland', published by the Government Printer in Brisbane in 1883. Bernays wrote that the olive had fruited well on coast lands near Brisbane and gave promise on the Darling Downs. He quoted a letter from Mr Davidson, station manager of the plantation 'Westbrook', formed by the late Dr Ricci: 'These trees, now six years planted, have grown exceedingly well, in height rather than thickness, some of them quite 10 feet high. This I consider a great growth, when it is allowed that the trees have had to pass through four most severe seasons of drought and one of the worst winters for frost ever remembered here, receiving during all this bad time no artificial watering help. Some of the trees fruited last year and a few this. The fruit appears to be of first-class quality, being well fleshed and of good size.' As time went by the trees suffered from mould. Sadly, only a few of these several hundred trees survive today.

Victoria's olive production had a series of stops and starts. The first Victorian olive trees were planted in the Wimmera area late in the nineteenth century. Two hundred trees planted at Longrenong College in the north-western district are still growing.

Kings were anointed with olive oil, which was believed to make them permanently sacred and inviolable. After anointment, the king would have it in his power to radiate peace, civilisation and wisdom. Olive oil became, with the crown, the embodiment of kingly authority.

In 1870 The Minister of Agriculture, 'Judge' Casey, who was an assertive and single-minded solicitor selected olives from France for Dookie College Farm, near Shepparton in Victoria's Goulburn Valley. The root truncheons arrived in two cases, packed in damp moss and wrapped in oil paper. *The Leader* newspaper of 7 June 1890 reported that, 'They were planted in nursery rows and not a single one failed to grow. The following year they were planted out and have been bearing.' The olive groves and manually operated knock down press have disappeared from Dookie Agricultural College, but John Newton Senior remembers them from when he was a student there in the 1930s. Under the supervision of the principal, A.C. Dreverman, the students harvested the olives and made the oil on site. The remains of the pressings were fed to the college pigs. Four gallon cans of the oil sold for eighteen shillings each.

In 1904 *The Leader* newspaper reported that Mildura was noted for its olive oil: 'The quality being exceptionally superior, and this industry promises to grow into one of large proportions.' Olive trees were planted in this area as shelter for the enclosed fruit trees and vines. According to the article, there was one olive oil factory in the area. Its annual output was expected to reach 1400 gallons that year, and 4000 gallons were expected when newly planted trees reached fruition.

Jacob Friedman planted a large number of olives at Horsham, Victoria, in the 1920s, near the Wimmera River in an area known as Riverside. Some of these trees are still growing today and are parent plants of the Verdallion variety. Friedman claimed that they were a strain of the Verdale he had selected himself.

P.J. Martin and J. Norman began buying olives in 1930 and pressing them for oil at Brighton, Adelaide, under the name Dover Olive Oil Mill.

Ancient Egyptians used to put large cones of perfumed ointment, often filled with olive oil, on their heads at dinner parties. As the atmosphere warmed up, the cones would gradually melt and drizzle scented oil over their bodies.

In 1941 they bought land at McLaren Vale, south of Adelaide, where they planted 3000 trees of Hardy's Mammoth, Sevillano, Gordal and Verdale varieties.

Just before the second world war, nine-tenths of the olive oil consumed in Australia was imported from Spain, Italy and France. Competition from this imported oil made it difficult for the Australian product to be developed into a profitable enterprise. During the war imported olive oil cost twelve pounds a gallon.

In 1942, Jacob Friedman, also known as the man who built Horsham's first picture theatre, set up a public company called the Grampians Olive Plantation with 800 shareholders. Sir Zelman Cowen's father, Mr Bernard Cowen, was one of the directors, as was Mr Chenoweth, Deputy Commissioner of Taxation, and a number of other prominent citizens, including Mr Garnett Carrol, the highly successful theatrical entrepreneur. Planting started in 1943 and by 1956, 43,000 olive trees had been established. The company planted as many varieties as possible because no one knew how each kind would perform. The origin of these olives is uncertain, but local history has it that a nursery in Barmera, South Australia, supplied many of the trees.

By 1959 the plantation had spent three million pounds. The Australian olive oil industry was in a slump – imported oil cost two pound five shillings a gallon – and the enterprise failed. This property is still virtually intact, unlike many of the other plantations around the area, which either no longer exist or have only a small percentage of the trees surviving.

The property changed its name to Toscana Olives in 1962 and installed an oil processing unit. A bumper harvest in 1966 looked promising but the oil could not be sold profitably. Geoff Winfield, the

Consecrated olive oil, in Jewish and Christian practice, represents the action of the Holy Spirit. Priests in the Catholic Church are ordained, as were priests in the Old Testament, by the pouring or rubbing on of olive oil.

present owner of Toscana, recalls: 'It took eight years to sell the oil. But what was produced was just oil, nothing more. It was comparable to the oil from Morocco and the southern part of Italy. The acid level was higher than our legal limits.'

Friedman had a falling out with the Grampians Company in 1948 and formed another company based on his 'mother plants'. He called it the Verdallion Olive Company. Friedman established 500 acres of new plantings at Mount Zero, five miles away from his original company, and 800 acres at Edenhope. The Verdallion Company supplied cuttings to a number of olive groves across the country.

Several other olive companies were established in the 1940s. One in Dimboola covered approximately 800 acres near the Little Desert. About 300 of these acres are still being farmed with difficulty. The other was SA Oils, a few miles out of Bordertown, which had 2500 acres of olives. The company folded in 1961, but there are 1000 trees left on the plantation.

The New Norcia monastery's Dom Serra and Dom Salvado spent much of their time moving between Perth, New Norcia, Guildford, Subiaco and Europe negotiating funds for the survival of their missionary work. They planted olive trees wherever they moved, and the Subiaco trees are still thriving and bearing fruit in what is now the Catherine McCauley Centre. The Sisters of Mercy settled in this area when they were asked to take over the orphanage. Even though the sisters were Irish, they appreciated the importance of olives and olive oil. They taught the orphans how to grow and treat the olives. The Sisters crushed the olives and pressed out the oil. Their excellent handling of olives won them first prize at the Perth Agricultural Show in 1954.

Migrants who came to Australia in great numbers after the second

Roman gastronomy was said to have achieved such a high degree of refinement that an experienced gourmet could tell with their eyes shut whether the olive they were eating had been picked with bare hands or by someone wearing gloves.

world war entered their new life through 'Bonegilla', an immigration centre for non-British migrants, opened by the Australian Department of Immigration in 1947. More than 300,000 people from all parts of the European continent passed through the gates of Bonegilla, which was located about eight miles from the nearest town of Albury.

For many of them, the food at 'Bonegilla' remains the most prominent memory of their first days in Australia. The fare consisted mainly of 'strange mutton, vegetables lifted out of water and sloshed on your plate, and then blasted with tomato sauce'. There was no sign of the olive oil, cured meats or cheese that many of them were accustomed to. Once settled in their new Australian homes, they had to be resourceful. Settlers in South Australia were pleasantly surprised to find Adelaide and its foothills covered in glorious olive trees, an unexpected heritage from British colonists.

There was little communication between the different migrant groups, and sometimes little within an ethnic group. Some Italians took the succulent olives they picked free of charge off the trees around Adelaide to the few traditional presses remaining from the colonial olive boom. Other migrants had to resort to buying their olive oil from the chemist at exorbitant prices in tiny bottles. Chemists were the main suppliers of olive oil until delicatessens started springing up around the country selling imported golden liquid in tins from Spain, Greece and Italy.

In the 1960s, Gilbert Sniel started a privately owned plantation at Hopetown in the Southern Mallee. Of the original 150 acres of trees, only thirty acres are standing today. At the same time, Francois Solente, a French Moroccan, planted his dream grove Kasbah near Loxton, in the Riverland. The grove was modelled on those of his homeland – densely planted trees

Jewellers traditionally polished their diamonds with olive oil. It was also the prime lubricant for the machines that powered the industrial revolution - 2000 years after it was used as axle grease by the Romans.

'I struggle to apprehend this. It is silver, perhaps a little blue, or perhaps somehow green - whitish bronze over reddish ochre earth. It is difficult, very difficult. Even so, it attracts me.'

Van Gogh

with multiple trunks. It now produces olive oil under the label Viva and is reputedly Australia's most productive grove.

H.E. Cuttle, with the financial support of R. Siddons, bought out a Soldier Settlement Board property at Robinvale in north-western Victoria in the 1960s. He planted 600 acres of olive trees at 'Oliveholme' which, unlike other groves, was irrigated. The property had its own olive press, but lack of technology and a slump in olive prices caused the property to fold in the 1970s. The press was later operated by the Meadowlea margarine company. Most of the grove fell to the bulldozer because the trees were not productive, but the grove is now being revived by a new owner.

According to Geoff Winfield, there were about 7000 acres of cultivated olives in Victoria by the 1950s. The Department of Agriculture appointed an olive advisor. But by the mid-1960s a lot of growers were starting to be pushed out. So much money was lost during that time that olives became a dirty word.

And from that time, until the great resurgence in the eighties, the olive industry was virtually dormant.

napoleon niarchos

Napoleon Niarchos was one of the many migrants who arrived in Australia from Greece in the 1950s. He had no knowledge of the grand colonial plans for olive production in South Australia when he arrived from a Greek village near Kalamata. He and his young family had fled from Greece during the civil war and, after passing through 'Bonegilla', and doing a stint labouring on the Nullarbor, they found themselves at the end of the railway line in Adelaide.

Napoleon, like many other Mediterranean migrants, brought his passion for olives with him to Australia. He was happy to discover that his new home was surrounded by healthy strong olive trees ready for the picking. Many of the trees had been neglected and were growing wild – paradise for this newly arrived Greek family.

Napoleon still reminisces about his homeland. His eyes brightened as he described the rolling hills of Kalamata covered in the silver-green mist of olive trees. Greece is the third largest olive producing country in the world after Spain and Italy, and its countryside is covered with over 120 million olive trees. As a child, Napoleon, and all the other village children, were allowed a few weeks off from school during the olive harvest. Families would band together to help each other. It was a golden time of singing and dancing and sharing.

Olive oil was greatly prized in Napoleon's home town, and involved temptation as well as joy and profit. Napoleon delights in telling the tale of the village priest who owned an oil factory. The priest rigged the hydraulic system so that he could siphon off half the oil from the villagers' olives for his own use. His devout congregation knew about his tricks but were powerless to do anything about them.

The villagers' olive trees were passed on from one generation to the next, and it was not unusual for a man to inherit one or two trees in another farmer's land. This led to feuds and in a few cases ended in murder. Such is the power of the olive.

Napoleon Niarchos now shares his enthusiasm with a growing band of olive lovers. His knowledge and ancient recipes are sought by many keen connoisseurs. Every year, like thousands of Greeks and Italians and ever more Australian converts, he picks his own olives, preserves them to be devoured by family and friends, and takes large sackfuls to be pressed into the golden liquid of his childhood.

Market gardener George Suttor brings the first olive tree to Australia • **1800**

Captain John Macarthur credited with introducing the olive tree
    to Australia • **1817**

Governor Stirling plants an olive tree at Parliament House, Perth • **1829**

The first olive tree arrives in South Australia from Rio de Janeiro
    on the Buffalo with Governor Hindmarsh • **1836**

Olive oil produced in Western Australia by Mr Jones of Woodbridge • **1843**

Olives imported to South Australia from Marseilles • **1844**

Benedictine monks plant olive grove at New Norcia monastery in
    Western Australia • **1846**

Mr Kid, the superintendent of the Sydney Botanic Gardens, produced
    the 'first oil in Australia' • **1847**

South Australian olive oil receives honourable mention at the
    London Exhibition • **1851**

Olives planted at Dookie Agricultural College, Victoria • **1870**

Stonyfell Olive Co Ltd established at Magill, Adelaide • **1873**

Adelaide Corporation plants 30,000 olive trees in Parklands • **1875**
Samuel Davenport has vision of a new Corfu between Adelaide
    and Kapunda

Olives planted on Westbrook station, Queensland • **1877**

1887 • Twenty-one-year leases granted in South Australia to encourage olive cultivation

1890 • Chaffey Brothers plant olive groves in the Riverina

1895 • Olive variety collection planted at Wagga Experimental Farm in New South Wales

1897 • Olive oil slump. South Australian oil stockpiled. Fifty cases shipped to Britain and given away to charities

1898 • New South Wales farmer at Berry uses olives as chook feed

1908 • New Norcia Lord Abbott Torres awarded Silver Medal for olive oil at Franco British Exhibition

1920 • South Australian Government approves an annual bonus of ten shillings an acre for ten years to anyone who plants olive trees

1942 • Grampians Olive Plantation with 800 shareholders established

1940s • Mediterranean migrants arrive to discover Adelaide, the Athens of the South, abundant with neglected olive trees

1959 • After spending three million pounds Grampian enterprise folds

1960s • French Moroccan, Francois Solente plants Kasbah near Loxton, SA

1970s • Greek and Italians privately producing their own oil in South Australia

1980s • The rest of the community discovers olive oil. Boutique olive oil labels established

1990s • The frenzy begins

In April 1997 the *Sunday Times* reported that the Greek island of Crete had Europe's healthiest population. In a development that could spawn a new fad for Cretan food, nutritionists had discovered that the islanders had far lower rates of heart disease, obesity and cancer than people in Britain and other European nations.

Cretans consume almost three times as much olive oil as northern Europeans, whose diet tends to be dominated by animals fats. Experts believe that olive oil brings optimum health because it provides a high intake of oleic acid, the monounsaturated fat that is found in the purest olive oil.

Tests by doctors and scientists at the European Commission – the executive arm of the European Union – show that replacing part of the animal fat content of a diet with olive oil can radically reduce levels of cholesterol, which can clog the blood stream. The doctors found that the greener and more virgin the olive oil, the higher the level of flavenoid chemicals which stop cholesterol deposits sticking to the artery walls. At the time of writing, they were finalising a dietary blueprint for circulation to all GPs in the European Union advocating the use of olive oil.

Olives provide small quantities of many nutrients including vitamin E, beta carotene, dietary fibre and minerals. Their oil is composed mainly of monounsaturated fatty acids which can lower blood cholesterol.

This information is not new. The World Health Organisation and Oldways Preservation and Exchange Trust have long supported the 'Traditional Healthy Mediterranean Diet Pyramid'. This recommends olive oil as the principal fat, replacing other fats and oils, including butter and margarine.

TO PREVENT A HANGOVER

Take a swig of the best olive oil before drinking alcohol.

Folk remedy

AS A GENTLE LAXATIVE

Take two teaspoons of olive oil before bedtime as a laxative and a shield against infection.

Folk remedy

There is probably no single factor responsible for the good health associated with Mediterranean diets. The diet has a high content of natural antioxidants from vegetables, legumes, fruits, nuts, red wine and olive oil. The protective factors in these foods, as well as the type and balance of fatty acids, may all be relevant.

For many years it was felt that polyunsaturates were the best for you as part of a low-fat diet to reduce the levels of cholestrol associated with heart disease, but in 1986 some new research into monounsaturated acids, in which olive oil is high, produced new evidence about the nature of cholesterol. It showed that contrary to earlier views there are actually two types: low-density lipoproteins and high-density lipoproteins. The low-density lipoproteins transport and deposit cholesterol in the tissues and arteries and increase with excessive consumption of saturated fatty acids. High-density lipoproteins, on the other hand, eliminate cholesterol from the cells. Polyunsaturated fats reduce both kinds of lipoprotein, but monounsaturates reduce low-density lipoproteins while increasing high-density ones. As the level of high-density lipoproteins increases, the levels of cholestrol decrease.

But olive oil is not just good for the heart. As well as containing up to 83 per cent monounsaturated fat, virgin olive oil is a natural food, rich in antioxidants and vitamins that help to prevent body cell aging, as well as giving the oil itself its conservation properties.

The body can produce most of the fatty acids found in foods but it cannot make either oleic acid or linolenic acid. These are essential fatty acids. Olive oil contains them both, making it an important and valuable dietary ingredient.

The nutritionist Rosemary Stanton writes that olive oil may do more than protect us from coronary heart disease. Some of the polyphenol antioxidants in olive oil may have the ability to destroy substances that lead to the proliferation of cells in the development of cancer. Further research is needed to establish how this protection occurs, but evidence shows that women in Mediterranean countries have much lower rates of breast cancer than those in countries such as the United States and Australia.

As well as its effects against coronary heart disease, and possibly breast cancer, the monounsaturated oleic acid in olive oil may have other beneficiary effects. Heart attacks occur when a blood clot blocks an artery that is already narrowed by fatty deposits. Some fatty acids are more likely to encourage clots than others. Oleic acid is one of the least thrombotic fatty acids. So oleic acid has advantages for health in terms of its effects on levels of undesirable low-density lipoprotein, cholesterol and on the possibility of clots.

There is some evidence that diabetes might be related to the kinds of fats within cell membranes and the way the membranes resist the action of insulin. An excess of the type of polyunsaturated fats found in many vegetable oils and most margarines compared with the type of poly-unsaturate fats found in fish and some vegetables may be a major problem. Using olive oil in preference to polyunsaturated vegetable oils would help provide a better balance of fats within cell membranes.

There are other reasons why olive oil is the preferred fat for diabetics. The usual advice to diabetics is to eat less saturated fat and substitute foods containing complex carbohydrate. If the complex carbohydrate foods are rich in dietary fibre, as occurs with whole-grain products, this advice may be fine – if the patients can stick to the diet.

Australian researcher Professor Kerin O'Dea has been comparing the

TO STRENGTHEN NAILS

Soak the nails in a warm solution of olive oil, then paint them with white iodine.
Folk remedy

TO PREVENT WRINKLES

Rub a mixture of olive oil and rosemary into the skin before going to bed.
Folk remedy

TO TREAT DRY SKIN

Make a paste of avocado and olive oil and rub into the affected parts. Leave for fifteen minutes then wash off.
Folk remedy

TO CLEAR SPOTTY SKIN

Rub the affected areas with a mixture of olive oil and some drops of rose oil.
Folk remedy

effects of different diets for people with diabetes. She has compared a diet rich in complex carbohydrate with one rich in monounsaturated fat from olive oil. Not only did subjects on the olive oil diet enjoy their food more, they also had better control of their diabetes and lower levels of some blood fats.

FOR TIRED TRAVELLERS

Massage the feet with warm olive oil.

Folk remedy

Eating a large amount of olive oil may keep you healthy but it will not keep you slim. Oil is 100 per cent fat and contains the same kilojoules as any other oil. But Professor Len Storlien and co-workers from the University of Wollongong are finding that different fats are used at different rates within the body. Some, such as stearic acid, which dominates meat and chocolate, are oxidised slowly and are therefore easily stored as body fat. Other fatty acids, such as oleic acid from olive oil, are poorly stored and are used up more quickly as an energy source. This doesn't mean that olive oil won't be converted to body fat, but it may make it less likely.

It is now not just the people of the Mediterranean who are discovering the nutritional and medicinal benefits of olives and their oil.

saturated fatty acids	mainly {	palmitic (7.5 to 20 per cent)
		stearic (0.5 to 5 per cent)
monounsaturated fatty acids	mainly {	oleic (55 to 83 per cent)
		palmitoleic (0.3 to 3.5 per cent)
polyunsaturated fatty acids	mainly {	linoleic (3.5 to 21 per cent)
		linolenic (1 per cent)
vitamin E	trace	
provitamin A (carotene)	trace	

golden
and
aromatic

'I was anointed with olive oil by the priest in the font of
the town's church, in the presence of my parents, uncles,
aunts and most of the town. And I grew up with olive oil in
my nose, mouth and pores, through my mother and grandmother's
cooking.' *Stefano Manfredi*

The olive blends powerful and perversely different tastes – acidic,
sweet, savoury and bitter. This magical and versatile fruit has become an indis-
pensible ingredient in contemporary diets – a far cry from its ancient origins as
a basic and accepted part of peasant fare throughout Europe and the Middle
East. The seemingly humble olive has entirely dominated food styles and
preparation wherever it has been cultivated. The different cuisines of the
Mediterranean are highlighted by the different ways that each region uses olives.
In eastern Mediterranean countries – Yugoslavia, Greece, Turkey, the Levant,
Egypt, and Libya – olives are used as garnishes and hors d'oeuvres. They are
also eaten like a fruit, often as small meals in themselves, accompanied by bread,

cheese and herbs. In the west – Tunisia, Morocco, Spain, Portugal, France and Italy – olives are often an ingredient in a recipe and cooked as part of it. Green olives are especially popular in these countries.

Just as the olive has reigned across a variety of nations and down through the centuries, so also does it appear comfortably at any part of a meal. Olives can be eaten at the beginning or end of a meal and, of course, they form the ingredients of many main courses; as well, they are an excellent accompaniment to drinks – the modern martini pays homage to the olive by including one 'swimming' in the glass. In Spain it is customary to end a meal with olives, and a person who arrives when the repast is over is said to 'get there with the olives'.

Olives are a feature of many of the traditional dishes of oil-producing countries. They impart taste and colour to salads, stuffings, gravies and sauces. They are used to garnish an endless array of meals and drinks, as well as being a condiment and appetiser. In some regions olives are prepared as a main dish because of their high nutritional value. The multitude of olive varieties and styles – green, black, stuffed, bruised, split – offer a whole range of culinary opportunites.

Olive oil is pure fruit juice, a gift from nature. It is free of additives and perfectly designed for human consumption. Unlike many other fat or oil products, which can be manufactured, olive oil can come only from olives. All efforts so far to extract the essential key to its flavour and in this way form the basis for a synthetic substitute have failed. Partly, no doubt, because of this amazing integrity, there are no fixed rules for using olive oil in cooking. Olive oil is a choice ingredient for vegetables and salads. But it is also delicious with fresh or toasted bread, and when used in dressings or as a seasoning. And it makes a glorious addition to casseroles, soups, meat and fish.

As well as having a unique taste, olive oil has flavour-enhancing properties, acting as a catalyst, and boosting the intensity of its companion ingredients. Commonly used for frying, olive oil makes food more succulent without detracting from its nutritional value. The food soaks up only a small amount of the oil because in the process an external, protective crust is formed. When drier foods are being fried – such as food coated in flour, eggs and bread crumbs – olive oil helps a crust to form. This crust keeps the temperature inside the fried food at about 100°C until the water inside the food has evaporated.

Smaller quantities of olive oil can be used for cooking at high temperatures. The oil increases in volume when subjected to heat, which explains why it is said that olive oil 'grows' in the frying pan.

The culinary uses of olive oil and the possibilities of its varied flavours are limited only by the cook's imagination. Just as wine buffs choose the most appropriate wine for each course, so olive oil connoisseurs will select the olive oil that is most suitable for the dish they are preparing.

shopping guide

olive oil

Shoppers should pay careful attention to the label when choosing a bottle of olive oil. This label might include olive variety, place of growth, harvesting details, extraction method and date, results of any analysis (at least the acidity), and results of any sensory assessment. Be cautious and understand that many oils bottled in Tuscany and Umbria in Italy are actually imported from Spain because the prestige of an Italian label adds greatly to the price of what may be an ordinary bottle of oil.

virgin olive oil

Virgin olive oil is obtained from the fruit of the olive tree by means that do not alter the oil at all. No solvents are used, no other oils are mixed with it, and it is not refined in any way. The olives are washed, crushed or milled and centrifuged, or pressed but that is all.

Virgin olive oil is graded according to its acidity in categories set down by the International Olive Oil Council – the International body of participating Nations responsible for the coordination of marketing of olives and olive oil worldwide – into extra virgin olive oil, fine virgin olive oil and ordinary virgin olive oil. Acidity of the oil is important because it reflects the care in the handling and processing of the fruit. The lower the acidity level, the better the quality of oil. Olive oil should be consumed within one year of harvest. Unlike wine, olive oil does not improve with age and it is preferable to buy a bottle of olive oil with a year of harvest or expiry date on the label.

extra virgin olive oil

Extra virgin olive oil is the purest form of olive oil. Ancient Greek olive groves were tended only by virgins, probably to ensure that the olives were not corrupted in any way, hence the name. Extra virgin olive oil has perfect taste and an aroma with an acidity level of no more than one per cent. It is the most expensive of all the oils.

fine virgin olive oil

This oil has minor imperfections of taste and aroma and a slightly increased acidity – but not more than 2 per cent.

ordinary virgin olive oil

This oil has a less than perfect taste and aroma, and an acidity between 2 and 3.3 per cent.

'pure' olive oil

This oil is a blend of virgin oil with lesser quality refined oil, and cannot be classified as a virgin olive oil.

first pressing

All olive oil labels must show the grade of oil in the bottle. The label may also carry the words 'first pressing' or 'first cold pressing'. This wording, which will only be found on bottles of extra virgin olive oil, means literally what it says – the bottle contains only oil from the first pressing. First cold pressed olive oil is utterly unaltered and retains its natural flavours.

cold pressing

The label may just carry the words 'cold pressing'. This means that the heat used to extract the oil has been kept to a minimum. If more heat is used, more oil will be extracted but it will be of a lower quality.

storing olive oil

Olive oil is best stored in dark glass bottles. Light will add to the natural deterioration of the oil. If oil is bought in plastic or tins, it should be decanted to coloured glass containers as soon as possible and stored in a cool dark place.

rancid oil

Oxidisation of the oil causes it to become rancid. The oxygen in the air gets into the oil container and is taken up by the fatty acid molecules. Oxidisation breaks down the oil, producing an unpleasant smell and taste. The less air contact with the oil, the better.

refrigerated oil

Olive oil should *not* be refrigerated as it may become thick and cloudy. If this happens, remove it from the fridge and it will return to normal.

flavour

It is impossible to tell what an oil will taste like by its colour. A darker, more intense colour does not necessarily mean more fruity flavour. The flavour and quality of olive oils can vary greatly.

If possible it is best to buy special oils from a provedore where you can taste before buying. If this is not possible, try buying a half bottle first so that you can decide if the olive oil is to your taste.

'I do not use Mediterranean oil because Australia does not always import the best quality olive oils from these countries.'
Ann Oliver

Olive oil has a great range of flavours. There are hundreds of different varieties of olive tree, many of which have more than one name. Some areas use local names for trees, but the same variety may have a different name when grown in another country or continent. This is further complicated by many trees being grafted onto different root stocks and grown in different climates or by different methods of cultivation.

The flavour, colour and aroma of olive oils differ according to where the olive trees are grown.

The taste of olive oils can also change from year to year depending on the weather.

French olive oils are light in taste and have great subtlety. They are sweet and gentle, but some producers say they lack the taste of the sun which is noticeable in oils from the more southern climates.

Italy produces some of the best olive oils in the world, particularly from the single estates. The oils are medium to heavy in weight and tend to be green in colour, with great complexities in taste. They range from the strongly assertive and peppery oils of Tuscany in the north, to the fruitier oils of Apulia in the south.

Spanish olive oils tend to be yellow and heavy, and they usually have a taste of the sun. Oils from the north often have a bitter almond taste; in the south, they are full of tropical fruit scents and flavours.

Greece produces oils that have a pronounced green colour and a medium weight. They do not have a vast complexity of taste but are extremely good value for money.

Greeks consume more olive oil per head than any other country – more than twenty litres a year!

Purveyor of quality foods Simon Johnson feels that the Australian olive oil industry is too young to have a national characteristic as yet. Australian olive oils are mainly made from table olives such as Kalamata, which, he says, have the same qualities of olives grown in Greece.

The oils are quite green and have a slight banana character with a

'I like using cloudy Greek olive oil: everything has not been filtered out of it.'

Irene Cashman

'Jane Ferrari's olive oil is the best Australian oil I have tasted.'

Stephanie Alexander

peppery edge. Simon believes that Australia will not have different varietals until oils are produced from individual varieties of olives. In time, and with the right cultivation and processing methods, he says, Australia will produce oils that will match the Italian single estates. He cites the Frantoio variety as an olive which would produce well in Australia.

olives

Flavours that go well with olives include fennel, fenugreek, cumin, oregano, bay leaves, rosemary, chilli peppers, and orange or lemon rind. Either vinegar or lemon juice may be added to the brine.

Olives vary greatly in size, shape, texture, and taste. Fresh olives are sold by colour, and this is determined by when they are picked. Green olives are picked early in the season and are inedible until they have been treated to remove the bitter glycosides; black olives are picked later when the fruit is fully ripe and will only need to be washed or preserved in brine or dry salt before being ready to eat.

In Australia, olives can be bought fresh from most markets from March to August. Black or green, they can be preserved using the recipes in this book.

preserved olives

Preserved olives can be bought from delicatessens, markets and specialised food stores. As they are pickled they don't need to be stored in the refrigerator. But if they are stoned it will not harm them. They should be returned to room temperature before serving.

There are many recipes for 'dressing' preserved olives. If time or motivation is a constraint, olives can often be bought already dressed.

black olives

Ripe black olives cannot be pitted because their flesh is too soft. Read the labels on bottles of imported black olives before you buy them. Some of

these imported olives are picked when green and then chemically blackened and the colour is then fixed with ferrous gluconate. There is no time for fermentation, which means that the olives will lack a strong pickled flavour. Unlike pickled olives, ripe black olives need to be sterilised at high heat so that they become resistant to spoilage.

green olives

Green olives have a bitter, tart flavour that is best complemented by acidic accompaniments and aromatic herbs.

feral olives

Feral or wild olives are a legacy of colonial plantings. Many feral trees are more than 100 years old. The fruit is usually very small and prized by enthusiasts for preserving.

'I love feral olives because of their intense flavour.' Maggie Beer

extra virgin oils

stefano manfredi

Stefano Manfredi only uses extra virgin olive oil, the oil's true form. He says that he would use extra virgin for everything if he could afford it, even for deep frying. He disagrees with the theory that extra virgin oil burns quickly, and scorns those who persist in the notion that to use extra virgin olive oil for cooking purposes is a waste of time and money.

Stefano, whose favourite Australian olive oil is Joe Grilli's Joseph Foothills, says that the best Australian oils come from trees in South Australia. His favourite oil is produced by Alfredo Mancianti in Umbria, Italy. Mancianti produces three oils, but Stefano's pick of the three is the Affiorato oil. This is a lighter and fruitier oil than those produced in the south of Italy, where the hotter climate produces a richer oil.

GREEN OLIVES

500 g green olives • 2 bay leaves, crumbled • 1/2 tspn fennel seeds • 1/2 tspn fresh thyme leaves • zest of 1 orange • 1 garlic clove • 1 tbspn olive oil Combine and marinate for 2 to 3 hours before serving. *Cath Kerry*

greek oils

zeffie kathreptis

Zeffie Kathreptis sometimes finds the Greek oil too strong for the palate. She thinks that the best olive oil is made when the olives are ripe but have not yet turned black.

italian oils

lew kathreptis

Lew Kathreptis has no particular favourite oil, though he generally prefers European varieties and in particular Italian olive oil. Like Stefano Manfredi, he believes that feral olives have more flavour and recommends Joe Grilli's oil. His favourite olives are the ones his father used to preserve.

veiled oils

rosa matto

Rosa Matto has a wardrobe of olive oils. As she changes her shoes to suit her outfits, so she changes her oil to suit her dishes. If she wants a refined flavour she uses Joseph Foothills; when she wants a more gutsy flavour, she uses the Joseph Extra Virgin. Rosa says that although the taste of Joseph olive oils varies, each vintage is consistently good.

When she wants a more rustic, earthy flavour, she uses the unfiltered oil she produces with her olive oil class – oil that is pleasantly inconsistent from year to year. This oil is now considered a 'veiled' oil rather than the less fashionable term 'cloudy' oil.

Rosa also uses Greek style olive oil when she wants to taste the olive fruit.

ferrari cold pressed extra virgin olive oil

stephanie alexander

Stephanie Alexander uses many different oils in her restaurant. She would, for example, use a free-flowing vegetable oil blended with a small amount of olive oil for deep frying, Spanish olive oil for general purpose sautéeing, or top of the range Bertolli for seasoning dishes. For special dishes where the flavour of the oil is part of the dish, she uses Colonna or any quality

Italian oil. She particularly favours oils from Umbria, Sicily and Tuscany.

Stephanie says that Jane Ferrari's olive oil is the best Australian oil she has tasted.

maggie beer
extra virgin
olive oil
maggie beer

Maggie Beer uses different grades of extra virgin, and says that it is only 30 per cent more expensive to buy a tin of extra virgin than to buy a tin of 'pure' olive oil. She believes that the name 'pure olive oil' should be removed from culinary vocabulary because the public mistakenly believe that pure olive oil is the best. She suggests that the different types be named extra virgin, virgin and olive oil.

Her favourite oils are Laudemio Dai Colli Della Toscana Centrale, Joseph Foothills, and, of course, her own brand. Although she has her own olive grove, Maggie loves feral olives because of their intense flavour, which, she claims, can be attributed to the age of the trees.

joseph foothills
chris manfield

Chris Mansfield tries all the new Australian olive oils as they come onto the market. She particularly likes the greenness and pepperiness of Joseph Foothills, and Jane Ferrari's oil. Chris appreciates the greenness in Greek oils, and imports a variety named Mani which is not available in the shops. She also uses a Spanish oil called Romanico.

Chris uses olives moderately in her cooking. She favours Kalamata, Ligurian and large green Spanish olives, and disapproves of the small black Spanish olives because of the preservatives used in them. Chris imports olives from the Pelopponese in Greece. These are packed in oil and are therefore soft when they arrive at Chris's restaurant, where she pickles them.

coriole

ann oliver

Ann Oliver's favourite oils are Joseph and Ferrari when she can 'get it from Jane'. She uses Coriole sometimes and keeps Joseph Foothills for special occasions. For general use she prefers the South Australian Olive Oil Company Extra Virgin. Ann points out that it is sometimes blended if there aren't enough South Australian olives available.

Ann does not use Mediterranean oils because she believes that Australia does not always import the best quality oil. Sometimes these oils sit for years on the shelf before they are bought.

new norcia

ian parmenter

Ian Parmenter enjoys the fullness and the pepperiness of Greek olive oil. He also likes the oil from New Norcia Monastery in Western Australia, but says that unfortunately it is rare. He likes to try new oils as they come on the market.

physical properties

solidification point	• 2°C
melting point	• 5 to 7°C
smoke point	• 210°C
weight	• 1 litre = 910 to 916 grams.

500 g olives = approximately 2¼ cups whole olives

500 g olives = approximately 2 cups stoned olives

125 g flour = 1 cup

Stefano Manfredi was born in the town of Gottolenga, between Brescia and Mantova. He says that just as olive oil fills every nook and cranny when the bottle holding it is dropped so Italian migration has successfully spilled the Italian sensibility about food to every corner of the globe. The great numbers of post-war migrants from the Italian peninsula have not only taken their families with them but also their culinary baggage.

Stefano Manfredi uses only extra virgin olive oil, an essential ingredient, which he says can stand alone, at his Rocks restaurant bel mondo. Respect for olive oil is almost religious today, he says: 'Olive oil reflects aspects of the place where the olives were grown – the soil, the climate – what the French call *terroir*. But you will only find the true expression of the land in traditional provincial pressed oils, not in the blended varieties.'

Olive oil, he says, brings connotations of a Mediterranean way of life where people live longer, are more relaxed, and eat simply. The peasant dishes of the Mediterranean satisfy the palate, the body and the spirit. People in Australia are trying to translate that into a modern way of life.

Stefano suggests using Italian cooking as a guide when it comes to using olive oil. Italy is a diverse country. In the south, Italians use olives in cooking, and the big rich oils are used with meat, tuna, and vegetables such as eggplant and capsicum. In the north, people eat a lot of beans, legumes, lake fish, and fresh water crays, and lighter oils are used.

What makes olive oil different from other oils, according to Stefano, is its diversity and expression of the land from which it comes. Other oils, such as grape seed and sunflower, are used by some cooks as a neutral medium through which food is cooked.

'Try stir-frying some Asian vegetables such as bok choy, een choy and Chinese cabbage in olive oil. Add a little garlic, and take to it with chopsticks. The results will be spectacular, especially if the vegetables are cooked in a wok and are left a little *al dente.*

'Olive oil is used because it tastes so good. Pizza without good olive oil is not worth considering. Bruschetta, requiring only the very best olive oil and crusty chunks of bread, has become popular because of its rustic simplicity and nostalgic flavours of a time when food was unrefined and wholesome.'

Stefano Manfredi is pragmatic about the Australian olive oil industry. He believes that Australian olive oil producers are making good but not great oils yet. He says that pride in the olive oil industry is justified but that, unlike the Australian wine makers, olive oil producers are rather insecure and the industry has yet to mature. Many people are ignorant about buying Australian oils, and he believes that producers should find out what kind of oils consumers want, using good Italian oils as their benchmark.

Warm salad of zucchini flowers, beans and roma tomatoes, with white truffle olive oil dressing

16 zucchini flowers with baby zucchini attached • 4 ripe roma tomatoes, quartered lengthways • ¹/₂ cup broad beans, double peeled • 200 g baby green beans, trimmed • young rocket leaves • ¹/₂ cup thinly shaved parmesan • 6 tbspn white truffle oil (terrabianca brand is very good) • salt and pepper to taste

Blanch zucchini flowers, broad beans and green beans separately until tender but still *al dente*. While still hot, toss this mixture in a bowl with tomatoes, rocket leaves and truffle oil. Season and arrange on plates, and finish with shaved parmesan on top.

Serves 4, first course

Pickled lettuce

As many varieties of lettuce as possible (radicchio, cos, iceberg, and so on, the tough outside leaves discarded) • whole cloves of garlic, crushed • red wine vinegar (the better the vinegar, the better the result) • extra virgin olive oil

Wash the lettuce leaves thoroughly, then place them in a pot and cover with water. Bring them to the boil, then simmer for 30 to 40 minutes until tender. Drain and allow to cool. Squeeze out excess water and arrange loosely in glass jars, placing crushed whole cloves of garlic every so often between the leaves. Cover the lettuce with red wine vinegar. Store in refrigerator or in a cool place for at least a week. To serve, squeeze out the excess vinegar, then chop the lettuce into small pieces, dress with extra virgin olive oil, and season.

Grilled long-tailed bugs with cannellini beans, tomato, olive oil and saffron sauce

PESTO

6 tablespoons chopped fresh basil leaves, 3 cloves peeled garlic, ¼ teaspoon salt, 3 tablespoons fresh grated parmesan cheese, 3 tablespoons chopped pine nuts, ¼ cup olive oil. Place chopped basil leaves, garlic and salt in a mortar and pound with a pestle until reduced to a thick paste. Stir in cheese, add oil, drop by drop, until the mixture has reached the required consistency.

2 kg roma tomatoes, peeled and mashed in a blender • pinch of saffron • ¹/₂ cup extra virgin olive oil • salt and pepper to taste • 20 long-tailed or moreton bay bugs • 1 cup cannellini beans, soaked overnight • additional olive oil • 4 tbspn pesto

Sieve the mashed tomatoes, then place them in a pot with the saffron. Heat the puree until it is almost boiling (but do not boil). Take it from the heat and whisk in the olive oil a little at a time until it is well incorporated. Season and allow to cool before using. Cook the beans in some salted water until they are *al dente*. Drain them and set aside.

Carefully take the bug tails out of their shells, using sharp kitchen shears. Rub olive oil over each tail and grill them, making sure they do not dry out or go crusty. They should be golden and moist.

Heat the tomato sauce and ladle a little onto each plate. Spoon beans in, put four or five bugs in the middle, and finish each dish with a spoon of pesto (see recipe this page).

Serves 4, main course

rosa matto

chef
adelaide

Rosa Matto's mother was one of the first women from her Italian village to come to Australia. She and her sister-in-law scoured the shops for olive oil. When they finally made it clear what they wanted, a shopkeeper sent them to a chemist, where they found bottles of rancid olive oil. Out of necessity they started to make their own: 'We first started making olive oil when I was a kid. My father was always embarrassed that someone might see us in the Adelaide parklands picking olives, so we usually went up to the hills. We always picked by hand and pegged up blankets beneath each tree because my mother wanted to soften the blow of the falling olives. We were supposed to catch any olives that fell in the baskets we had strapped around our necks. My mother would have an extra bucket for the absolutely ripe olives, which she would cook in olive oil and sprinkle with plenty of sea salt as a treat for us when we got home. The olives still had a certain bitterness, but they were delicious. I narrowly missed death when I was about seven. I lost my footing and slipped. We were on a cliff face and I started to run down the hill; I couldn't stop myself. My parents were yelling at me to sit down, but I couldn't stop moving, let alone sit down. I finally crashed into a tree. I've been terrified of picking olives ever since.'

For the past seven years Rosa has been making olive oil in her cooking school. Not surprisingly, one of her criteria is that the olive trees are on flat ground! When students in her classes first started picking olives, they were allowed to go anywhere. Rosa recalls visiting a dairy farm, where the students chopped away the undergrowth and did a minimal amount of pruning during the year. The farmer thought they were lunatics. He could have any amount of the oil he wanted, but he only ever accepted one bottle which he would struggle to finish within the year. The last year they approached him, the farmer said that lots of people has asked him if they could pick his olives and he had decided to charge. In seven years, Rosa's olive oil producing students, no longer lunatics, had become respectable.

When Rosa was growing up her family had a selection of oils.

'At home we had the good olive oil, then we had the good oil mixed with some not so good oil to make it go further for everyday use. We also bought vegetable oil which we would use for frying, but we never blended that with the olive oil. Whatever olive oil we had was given to us, and it had to last the whole year, so we saved it for special occasions. We found that the full on extra virgin flavour was too strong for certain dishes so we used the one we had blended. For bread and salads we used the good oil. We always consumed the entire contents of the bottle within a year so that there was no remaining oil to go rancid.'

At Rosa Matto's cookery school they pick the olives one day and press them the next. Rosa insists that for purity and cleanness of taste the olives must be pressed as soon as possible after picking. When she put her hand into one of the bags of picked olives and pulled it out warm and oily, Rosa concluded that olives generate their own heat.

Rosa believes that you should use whatever you are comfortable with – she uses olive oil for just about everything: 'People still talk about extra virgin oil being sacrosanct. They talk about it in hushed whispers. If people are marinating sun-dried tomatoes, there is no way they should use extra virgin oil. It would be a waste of time and money because so much flavour would be imparted to the oil. It is really a question of what the dish is intended to be in the end. Most people need to buy half bottles of new oils first to see what they like.'

In Rosa's view, olive oil is now a fashionable commodity in Australia, but for all that there is no understanding of its culture or the economy of its use. 'People are now embracing olive oil with the same passion as wine,' she says.

Rosa thinks that olive oil tastings are enlightening and entertaining, but that so far no one in Australia has developed a grammar and vocabulary to articulate the flavours and describe the effects of different oils on the palate. Most people believe that any olive oil is wonderful and as a result do not analyse what they like and dislike about it. She is full of hope that, with tutoring, those talents will develop here.

Rosa herself is one of the authorities who can provide us with the kind of analysis, advice and survey that will gradually produce an olive oil literacy in Australia just as there is a highly sophisticated wine literacy: 'Oils will change from year to year,' she says. 'If an oil producer wants to have consistency year in, year out, they have to doctor their oils. That can be a dangerous thing. We have to insist that every bottle has a date on it.' In her view, Australians need to keep talking about olive oil to establish a vocabulary to describe what they are tasting. The European vocabulary for olive oil manufacturing does not suit Australia: 'As well as the international oil language, Australians could have oil that is "cactus". Then everyone would know if an oil is off,' she jokes.

Rosa claims that some Australian producers are expecting too much from every batch of olive oil and are selling it while it is too young or too old: 'Newly pressed oils need to sit for three months in new tins. It should then be bottled and can be used straight away. We keep the sediment in our oils, filter them through coffee paper and then decant them. They are fine. A lot of people say that if you filter the oil you filter out a lot of the flavour. Some say that if you keep an oil unfiltered it will last for a longer period of time.'

Rosa is used to some olive oil being 'cloudy' but claims that this is no longer accepted nomenclature. Cloudy olive oil is now called 'veiled', and when it is 'veiled' it is a good thing. She realises that when people say that an oil is rancid, they are often tasting over-ripe fruit. Rancid oil has a very musty taste.

rosa matto's
recipes

Goat's cheese terrine with green olive pesto

400 g fresh goat's cheese • fresh marjoram, chopped • 2 tbspn olive oil • 150 g green olives, stoned • 2 anchovy fillets • 50 g capers • juice of half a lemon • juice of half an orange • zest from both lemon and orange, finely chopped

To make the olive pesto, work the cheese with the marjoram and oil until you have a smooth paste. Puree the olives, anchovies, capers, juices and zest. Line a terrine with plastic film. Place a layer of cheese, then a layer of the pesto, and finish with more cheese. Cover and weigh down overnight. Serve with polenta chips and an olive oil dressing.
Serves 8

Insalata di broccoli con pinoli (broccoli salad with pinenuts)

1 bunch broccoli • 125 ml olive oil • 2 cloves garlic, chopped • chilli (amount depends on personal taste and strength of the chilli) • small handful pine nuts, lightly roasted in hot oven

Cut broccoli into flowerettes and blanch in salted water. In a frypan heat olive oil until it is warm. Add garlic, chillies and pine nuts. While the broccoli is still warm, pour the dressing over and toss.
Serves 6

Funghi sott'olio (marinated mushrooms)

$3^1/_4$ cups white wine vinegar • $^1/_2$ cup white wine • 1 cup water • 4 bay leaves • salt to taste • 1 kg mushrooms, wiped clean • olive oil • 4 cloves garlic, cut in halves

In a large saucepan, bring the vinegar, water and wine to the boil. Add bay leaves, salt and mushrooms. Bring to boil again and simmer for 5 to 6 minutes. Drain mushrooms on a wire rack, stem-side down. Sterilise a jar or two and pour some olive oil into them. Put in a layer of mushrooms, 1 bay leaf and half a clove of garlic, cover with oil, and continue until the jar is full. Press vegetables down with the back of a spoon so that no air is trapped. Oil must cover the final layer of vegetables. They will keep for months providing no air is able to affect them. Use marinated mushrooms as part of an antipasto platter. The marinade can also be used for red peppers, asparagus, French beans, or other vegetables.

Penette alla rucola fresca

4 handfuls rocket, stemmed • 4 cloves garlic, finely chopped • $^1/_2$ tspn dried chilli flakes • 6 tblspns olive oil • 500 g penette or other short pasta • black pepper to taste

Place garlic, chilli and olive oil in a small pan. Sauté for 2 to 3 minutes. Meanwhile, cook the pasta in salted water. Drain. Toss with sauce and freshly ground black pepper. Add the rocket and a few extra drops of olive oil. Serve with grated parmesan cheese.

Serves 6, first course

Pasta with fennel, raisins and tomato – sicilian style

3 bulbs fennel • 1 clove garlic, finely chopped • olive oil • $^1/_2$ cup raisins, soaked in $^1/_2$ cup water • 1 tin tomatoes, peeled (do not drain but chop roughly) • salt and pepper to taste • rosemary to taste • 500 g penne, spirali or fusilli • parmesan cheese, freshly grated • 200 g black olives

Slice the fennel and sauté in the olive oil. Add garlic and cook until the fennel is soft. Add tomato and cook for 10 minutes. Sprinkle in drained raisins and rosemary to taste and then adjust seasoning, remembering that olives will garnish the dish. Meanwhile, cook the pasta and drain. Toss with sauce and serve with parmesan and black olives.

Serves 6, first course

Tagliatelle alle olive 250 g field mushrooms, thinly sliced • 10 g porcini mushrooms, soaked (retain the soaking water) • 3 tbspn olive oil • 1 clove garlic, finely chopped • salt to taste • $1/4$ tspn chilli pepper • 100 ml cream • 500 g tagliatelle • 50 g parmesan cheese, freshly grated

Lightly fry the mushrooms in oil until tender, then blend with garlic, olives and parsley in a food processor. (This mixture will keep for one week in the fridge.) Cook tagliatelle until *al dente*. Meanwhile, heat the olive mixture, adding salt and chilli pepper and incorporating the cream. Mix with tagliatelle and serve with parmesan. The idea is to dress the pasta with the sauce, not to drown it.

In Umbria, where this dish originates, it is usual for the cream to be left out of the cooking and for a bowl of whipped cream to be served alongside the parmesan.

Serves 6, first course

Fettucini con prosciutto, pomodori e olive cherry tomatoes • kalamata olives • whole cloves of garlic • rosemary • black pepper to taste • olive oil
fettucini: 500 g fettucini (allow 100 g per person for a first course) • salt to taste • 200 g prosciutto • pine nuts, lightly roasted in oven • parmesan, shaved not grated • best

quality olive oil • small quantity chilli, chopped • 2 cloves
garlic, left whole

Braise the olives, whole cloves of garlic, rosemary and black pepper in olive oil at 200°C until the olives are slightly wrinkled (about 20 to 30 minutes). Add the tomatoes and bake until they begin to collapse (about 10 minutes). Using a slotted spoon, remove the olives and tomatoes from the oven, discarding the rosemary and garlic. Keep the flavoured oil for a salad or to brush on chicken or bread before grilling.

To prepare the fettucini: in a large quantity of boiling, salted water, cook the pasta. Meanwhile, heat the olive oil and cloves of garlic. Just as the garlic colours, remove and discard it. Lightly fry the prosciutto, then add the olives, tomatoes and chilli. Drain the pasta and toss it in a bowl with the prosciutto mixture. Add the roasted pine nuts. Pile the pasta on plates and cover with parmesan and cracked pepper.

Serves 6, first course

1 cup black olives, pitted • 200 g potato, cooked and mashed • **Olive bread**
500 g bread flour • 1 cup olive oil • 200 ml water •
20 g compressed yeast, dissolved in 1 tspn sugar and 100 ml
warm water

Allow the yeast, sugar and water to form a 'sponge'. Then combine with other ingredients (you can use a food processor); knead on a floured surface. Put into a bowl, covered in a warm place for an hour or until doubled. Knock down and knead very lightly. Put in oiled pans and allow to double again. Bake at 210°C for 40 to 50 minutes. Cool on rack.

Makes 2 loaves

Pesce in carpione (marinated tommy ruffs)

1 kg small fish fillets (tommy ruffs, mullet or garfish) • flour • vegetable oil

marinade: 8 tbspn olive oil • 2 onions, sliced • 3 cloves garlic, sliced • 1 tbspn white sugar • 2 glasses white wine vinegar • 1 glass white wine • 4 bay leaves • 1 sprig fresh rosemary • salt to taste • 1 tbspn whole peppercorns

Roll the fish in flour so that it is dusted on all sides. Heat vegetable oil in a frying pan and fry the fish on both sides until golden brown. Drain on kitchen paper. Heat the olive oil in a saucepan and fry the onions until soft. Add slices of garlic, sugar, vinegar, wine, bay leaves, rosemary, salt and peppercorns. Bring to boil then remove. Place fish fillets side by side in a shallow dish. Pour hot marinade over and leave for 24 hours before serving.

Serves 4, main course

Grilled chicken with green olive dressing

chicken: • 1 lemon • 250 g chicken thigh fillets, cut into chunks • 8 tblspns olive oil • 2 cloves garlic, peeled and crushed • salt and pepper to taste

dressing: 2 anchovy fillets • 175 g pitted and finely chopped green olives • 1 clove garlic, minced • $1/2$ cup fresh parsley, chopped • 4 tbspn lemon juice • zest of 1 lemon, finely chopped • salt and pepper to taste

garnish: black olives • 4 lemon wedges • parsley leaves

Marinate the chicken meat with the zest from the lemon, 2 tablespoons of the olive oil, garlic, salt and pepper for 2 hours or overnight. (If marinating longer than 2 hours, leave out the salt.) Make the dressing by working

the anchovies, olives, minced garlic, parsley, lemon juice and zest with the rest of the oil in a food processor until the mixture has a chunky salsa consistency. Season with salt, pepper and more lemon juice if needed.

Skewer the chicken. Grill, preferably over charcoal. Remove the skewers and toss the chicken with the dressing. Serve warm or at room temperature garnished with lemon, parsley leaves and black olives.

Serves 4, first course

Endive pie

bread dough: 300 g plain flour • salt to taste • 20 g fresh yeast, dissolved in 1 cup tepid water • 30 g lard

filling: 1.5 kg green leafy vegetables: witlof, endive, spinach or lettuce • garlic, chopped • olive oil • $^1/_2$ cup sultanas or raisins • 2 tbspn capers, chopped • 10 anchovy fillets • 30 g pine nuts • salt and pepper to taste • 175 g black olives, pitted and chopped

Bring together all the bread dough ingredients and knead for a few minutes. Allow to double in volume (this will take about 30 minutes).

To prepare the filling: cook the washed leaves for 20 minutes, drain and squeeze out moisture. Sauté chopped garlic in oil, then add leaves, stirring occasionally. Add the sultanas and capers and rapidly boil away any liquid. Allow to cool then add anchovies, black olives and pine nuts. Check for salt and pepper.

To assemble the pie: grease a 250 mm round shallow tin. Divide the bread dough into 2 parts, one twice the size of the other. Roll out the larger piece to cover the bottom of the tin. Line its sides and leave some hanging over to seal the pie. Then put in the filling. Roll out the remaining piece of dough. Cover the top of the pie, pressing the edge of the lid against the dough lining the tin, bringing the top sheet over, and lightly sealing with fingers. Cook for 45 minutes at 190°C. Cool on rack. Serve lukewarm or at room temperature.

stephanie alexander

richmond
hill cafe
and larder

melbourne

Stephanie Alexander believes that the resurgence of olive oil is related to migration and fashion. She claims that its appeal has reached beyond the traditional ethnic group because of the influence and proliferation of food writing. A food must have media cache before it is taken up, she says, and the image of olive oil is well served in this by members of the food press who have helped us to understand just how good it is. Olive oil is now being embraced with an evangelistic passion.

Stephanie's mother, a fabulous cook, used olive oil. She was especially proud of her olive oil mayonnaise. Stephanie has been using olive oil on a daily basis since the 1970s. She remembers that, during her student days, the University Cafe in Lygon Street had a cruet of olive oil and vinegar on every table for individual salad dressing. She had thought at the time that the idea was incredibly sophisticated.

Stephanie recognises that olive oil is a way of life for many people in the world: 'Every country has its everyday olive oil and its Sunday best. We shouldn't get hooked on all the hype. We aren't required to use the finest estate bottles. The more people are told to use these, the more these oils are put out of their reach. We can't afford to pay those prices.

Olive oil is perfect for warm salads where butter shouldn't be used, she says. She also uses olive oil for a sophisticated and delicious finish for simple foods such as grilled fish. Stephanie recognises that olive oil and fresh herbs complement each other well, and particularly likes olive oil with parsley, chives, and rosemary, and sometimes with sage, salad leaves, anchovies and other salty foods like capers.

Preserved olives have always been a part of life for Stephanie. She is not keen about using olives for stuffing, as they can be overpowering, but she recommends using them with rabbit and chicken. She thinks that the best Australian oils are very exciting, and that they are well made and have good character. But she acknowledges that people who are looking for the best qualities of Italian oils won't find them in the Australian product. Stephanie believes that part of the appeal of olive oil is its complexity of flavour, not just its oiliness. She says that so far a lot of Australian oils lack complexity.

Stephanie admits modestly that she hasn't studied olive oil enough to make fine distinctions between all the nuances involved in olive tasting. But she is not sure that the Australian olive oil industry is capable of great flavour variation. Cynical of the way new products are taken up then dropped suddenly, Stephanie believes that, in Australia, olive oil is here to stay. She says that endorsement by the Heart Foundation and marketing clout of the big olive oil companies have seen to that: 'People should just enjoy olive oil without carrying on about it having an almond or apple flavour or being peppery. It's delicious and makes cooking easy, and that's what it is all about. With olive oil and a non-stick pan and a piece of fish you can have dinner on the table in ten minutes. By all means use special oil over a piece of fish or a piece of parmesan. But we shouldn't intimidate people.'

Fetta and olives   Sprinkle the finest sheep's milk fetta cheese with extra virgin olive oil mixed with some very finely chopped garlic and thyme leaves and enjoy with fat, oily black olives.

Marinated olives   black olives • olive oil • cumin seeds, toasted • raw fennel or celery, finely diced • chilli and garlic, finely chopped • fresh bay leaf or thyme leaves • fresh parsley, coarsely chopped • preserved lemon, finely diced

Combine and marinate several hours before serving.

Ajo blanco
(white gazpacho
from malaga)   125 g sourdough bread • 250 ml milk • 60 g blanched almonds • 2 cloves garlic, crushed • pinch of salt • 200 ml extra virgin olive oil • 2 tbspn best spanish sherry vinegar • 2 cups water
garnish: 100 g sourdough bread, cut into cubes • 2 tbspn olive oil • 125 g grapes, peeled and seeded

Soak bread in milk. In a food processor, work almonds, garlic and salt to a paste. Add milk-soaked bread and blend well. With motor running slowly, add oil, stopping to scrape the bottom of the bowl two or three times. The consistency should be that of a thick mayonnaise. Remove to a bowl and slowly whisk in the vinegar and water. Check for seasoning. Refrigerate for several hours.

Fry cubed bread for garnish in oil and drain well. Whisk soup again, ladle it into flattish bowls, and drop a handful of grapes into each bowl. Garnish with croutons.

Serves 4

600 g strong flour • 150 g stoned black olives, halved • 2 tspn salt • 1 tbspn instant dried yeast • 2 tspn finely chopped fresh rosemary • 4 tbspn olive oil • 300 ml warm water • sea salt as required

Olive bread, olive foccacia, and olive and grape bread

Mix flour, olives, salt, yeast and rosemary in a large bowl. Add oil to water. Make a well in the flour and tip in liquid, then stir to mix well. Tip onto an oiled workbench and knead with oiled hands for 15 minutes (or transfer to an electric mixer fitted with a dough hook) until dough is springy and elastic. Place dough in a lightly oiled bowl, cover with a clean tea towel and leave in a draught-free place to double in size (about 45 minutes). Tip dough gently onto workbench. Do not knock back. Work into a cigar-shaped loaf with oiled hands, then place on a floured tea towel and allow to rise again for 30 minutes. Preheat oven to 220°C with a baking tray in it. Roll loaf onto tray, scatter with flakes of sea salt and bake for 20 minutes (there is no need to mist the oven with water). This bread is particularly good served slightly warm. Green olives may be substituted for black. You can also add chopped semi-dried tomatoes or slightly crispy bacon.

For olive focaccia: transfer the dough after the first rising to an oiled baking tray and flatten with oiled hands into a rectangle 2 to 3 cm thick. Scatter with flakes of sea salt and drizzle with a little olive oil. Allow to recover for 30 minutes, then bake at 250°C until browned and crisp.

For grape and olive bread: knead lightly crushed grapes and chopped young grapevine leaves and tendrils into risen olive bread dough. Press dough onto a pizza tray with well-oiled hands and allow to recover for 10 minutes. Drizzle with olive oil, scatter with sea salt and bake at 250°C until crisp. Serve with fresh ricotta.

maggie beer

chef

barossa valley

Maggie Beer admits that she has been seduced by olive oil. She started to use it in the early 1980s when she was exploring Mediterranean food because of the similar climate of the Mediterranean and South Australia. Her friends joked that she should have called her restaurant 'The Olive Tree' rather than 'Pheasant Farm': 'Ten years ago there was only a handful of chefs who revered olive oil. Marketing by the International Olive Oil Council targeted food writers, and they have changed public opinion. It was a blatant and commercial strategy, but it was very successful. It was also two-pronged – the aficionados were driven by flavour, and the public was open to education. Our chefs are changing now, and flavour is driving people more than technique.'

Maggie adores the variety, depth and complexity of flavour that olive oil possesses, and the different nuances from different areas. She appreciates the versatility of olive oil and that in its different guises the oil has a broad range of uses: 'Used simply there is nothing better than olive oil in the kitchen. The other night I had some freshly caught yabbies with salt, olive oil and lemon juice – divine. You could taste the oil, taste the flavour. Other oils such as canola and safflower are a lubricant rather than a source of flavour. Other great oils – walnut, hazelnut, almond – have to be used very specifically. With olive oil you have the whole gamut, you can use it for so much more.'

Maggie does not use olive oil for Japanese cooking. In her kitchen, olive oil is used purely for Mediterranean cuisines. She uses different grades of extra virgin oil. Maggie buys imported four-litre tins of extra virgin for 'ordinary stuff', such as brushing kangaroo steaks and sweating onions. She loves the 'mouth feel' of good quality olive oil and uses the best oil for drizzling over hot foods and on the table. Maggie Beer always uses a bottle of oil and a bottle of vinegar on the table for salad dressings, because people have individual preferences on the ratio of oil to vinegar in a dressing.

As a member of the Australian Olive Association, Maggie is very involved in the resurgent Australian olive industry. She believes that Australia has the opportunity to do wonderful things with its olive oil, provided there is an emphasis on quality: 'Pride in Australian olive oil is not enough. You have to have the quality at a reasonable price. We are yet to find the right varieties for the right areas, and we don't have enough good crushing facilities. We don't have the knowledge of when and where to pick. It is a long process and every link in the chain must be perfect. Late-picked olive oil won't last as long as the early picked oil. We have no longevity in our oils in Australia because we don't have our quality right yet. It is a time for experimentation. Some trees will be successful, some won't. You have to be in the business for the long term. It's not a short-term fix of agricultural economics. We are starting from scratch with a clean, green environment. There is no excuse for olive cultivators to make mistakes.'

Maggie Beer admires the energy of the Australian olive industry but emphasises that growers should not lose their strength. She recommends trial plantings to get things right. She realises that there is a long way to go, but that the journey has already begun.

SALTED (PRESERVED) LEMONS

Allow 2 teaspoons of salt for each large lemon. How you cut your lemon depends on how long you are prepared to wait for them and how you want them to look. Cut lemons into eight wedges and layer them with salt in a sterilised jar with salt *or* cut them into quarters, keeping the base intact so as to preserve the appearance of whole lemons. Place in a sterilised jar with salt. The addition of other herbs in the pickling jar is optional (and to some extent purely decorative). After 24 hours the jar should be three-quarters full of lemon juice, then add enough squeezed lemon juice to cover. Use after three weeks. 'Whole' lemons need a little longer. When a recipe calls for preserved lemons, discard the flesh and use only the peel.

Cath Kerry

She also believes that the Australian palate needs to be educated about olive oils in the same way that our wine palates have been developed. She suggests that uninitiated people taste oils before they spend their money on expensive purchases. In her view good provedores should offer people a chance to taste before they buy.

maggie beer's
recipes

Mayonnaise

2 large free-range egg yolks (at room temperature) • pinch maldon sea salt • 1 tspn dijon mustard • 250 ml mellow extra virgin olive oil or half extra virgin, half vegetable oil • 1 to 2 tbspn lemon juice • freshly ground black pepper to taste • 1 tbspn boiling water (optional)

Rinse a bowl with hot water and dry it thoroughly. Whisk the egg yolks with a pinch of salt until thick, then add the mustard and whisk until smooth. Continue whisking and add the oil drop by drop (until you are a confident mayonnaise-maker do this painfully slowly!). Once the mixture begins to thicken, add the oil in a slow, steady stream, whisking continuously. When the mayonnaise is established, add the lemon juice a little at a time. Taste for seasoning, then add the boiling water if the mayonnaise needs thinning and requires no more acidulant.

Anchovy and olive butter

Quail is fantastic with this butter, as are grilled lamb chops, rabbit and roo.
6 anchovy fillets • 150 g black olives • 150 g softened butter • good dash of brandy

Chop the anchovies and stone the olives, then mix both in a food processor. Add the butter and blend again to incorporate well. Form the butter mixture into a log, then wrap it in foil or plastic film and chill.

gnocchi: 500 g cooked potatoes • 2 egg yolks • 125 g plain flour • 20 large green olives, stoned and chopped finely • freshly grated nutmeg to taste • salt and pepper to taste

sauce: 1 large onion, finely chopped • 3 cloves garlic, finely chopped • 1 tbspn olive oil • 100 ml cream • juice of 1 lemon • 100 ml chicken stock • 200 g green olives, stoned and chopped

Green olive gnocchi with green olive sauce

To make the gnocchi: steam the potatoes until cooked right through and mash while still keeping warm. Allow to cool and add flour, nutmeg, salt and pepper, and chopped olives. Mix in the egg yolks until the dough is fairly firm, and knead it gently for a few minutes. While the salted water comes to the boil, shape the gnocchi dough into your desired form. Leave to rest. Gently place the gnocchi into boiling water and, after they rise to the surface, allow them to cook for 1 minute. Take out with a slotted spoon and put aside.

To make the sauce: sweat the garlic and onion in olive oil until wilted. Add chicken stock and cream and reduce to desired thickness. Add olives and adjust with lemon juice if necessary. Allow to cool a little and then puree in blender.

To serve: pan fry the gnocchi in some nut brown butter and serve with heated sauce.

Serves 6, first course

Skate with capers and olives

Skate, the wings of a stingray, is generally inexpensive. In some states it is sold untrimmed with the skin on, so it may need to be cleaned before cooking.

4 x 225 g skate • freshly ground black pepper to taste • plain flour • 2 cloves garlic • extra virgin olive oil (as required) • 1 handful flat-leaf parsley • 4 tbspn capers • 4 tbspn stoned and sliced black olives • 4 tbspn verjuice • squeeze of lemon juice

Preheat oven to 180°C and trim the skate of skin if this has not already been done by your fishmonger. Season the flour. Finely chop the garlic and brown it in 4 tablespoons of olive oil in a larger oven-proof, heavy-based frying pan, being careful not to burn it. Dust each piece of skate with the seasoned flour and brown it in the pan with the garlic for about 2 minutes a side, depending on thickness. Remove the stems from the parsley (don't throw them out) and chop the leaves (you need about 2 tablespoons of chopped parsley). Add the parsley stems with the capers, olives, verjuice and lemon juice to the pan with the skate, then season.

Transfer the pan to the oven and bake for 4 minutes, then turn the skate over and bake for another 2 minutes. Toss the skate with the parsley leaves on a warmed serving platter, then drizzle on a little extra virgin olive oil. Reduce the sauces in the pan over heat and pour over the fish. Serve with boiled waxy potatoes.

Serves 4, main course

VERJUICE

Verjuice originated in Roman times. It is made from unripened white grapes. It is an acidulant milder than lemon juice or white wine vinegar, and, when used doesn't mask the flavour of the food to which it has been added. Maggie Beer Verjuice is available from selected specialty food shops.

2 kg chicken thighs • 24 black olives • 2 preserved lemons •
1 tbspn fennel seeds • extra virgin olive oil as required •
freshly chopped flat-leaf parsley • salt and freshly ground
black pepper to taste

Chicken pieces roasted with olives, preserved lemon and fennel

Trim the meat of any excess fat. Stone the olives and slice the preserved lemons, then toss with the chicken and the remaining ingredients. Leave the chicken to marinate for 1 to 2 hours. Preheat the oven to 250°C. Place the chicken and its marinade in a heavy-based baking dish, making sure none of the pieces overlap and there is just enough oil to coat everything. Grind the pepper over the chicken and roast for 10 minutes, making sure the marinade ingredients are not burning. Turn the temperature down to 180°C and cook for another 10 minutes. Remove the dish from the oven and allow to rest, covered, for 15 minutes. Check for seasoning, then drizzle more olive oil over and garnish with lots more parsley. Serve with polenta or pasta. Serves 6, main course

This succulent slow-cooked dish can also be made with
kangaroo tail.
3 large onions • 2 sticks celery • 125 ml extra virgin olive
oil • 115 g shelled walnuts • 4 kg oxtail, cut into 5 cm
pieces • salt and freshly ground black pepper to taste •
plain flour • 100 g butter • 500 ml red wine • 4 cloves garlic
• 10 stems parsley • 2 sprigs thyme • 2 bay leaves •
500 g fresh or canned, seeded and peeled tomatoes • 2 litres
veal stock • 4 strips orange zest • 40 black olives •
125 ml red wine vinegar • 4 tbspn sugar

Oxtail with orange, olives and walnuts

POLENTA

Polenta (corn meal) can be used when just made, or it can be allowed to cool, then sliced and grilled or fried.

Tradtional recipe

1.75 litres water •
200 g coarse polenta •
salt to taste
Put the water into a broad, heavy-bottomed sauce pan and bring to the boil.
Add the salt, then add the polenta in a thin trickle, beating it into the water with a whisk. Lower the heat to medium and stir with a wooden spoon. Cook, stirring constantly for 40 minutes, or until the polenta comes away from the sides of the pan. Moisten the inside of a large bowl with water and turn the polenta into the bowl.
Let it rest for 5 minutes, then turn the polenta onto a large flat dish
serves 6

Preheat the oven to 200°C. Chop the onions and celery and toss with a little of the oil in a baking dish, then roast for 20 minutes until caramelised. Dry-roast the walnuts in the oven on a baking tray for 6 minutes, then rub their skins off with a clean tea towel and set aside.

Trim the oxtail of any fat. Toss the meat in seasoned flour and shake off the excess. In a heavy-based frying pan, brown the oxtail in batches in the remaining oil and butter. Put each batch in a large, heavy-based casserole. Add white wine to the frying pan to take up all the caramelised bits from the browning. Mince the garlic and add it with the onion, celery, and herbs and tomatoes to deglaze the pan. Reduce it a little, then tip the lot into the casserole. Add the veal stock, making sure everything is covered, and simmer, covered, until tender. This could take 3 to 4 hours. Add the orange zest and olives in the last 20 minutes of cooking.

Strain the cooking juices from the meat and remove as much fat as possible from the top. Set the meat aside in a warm place. In a stainless steel or enamelled saucepan, combine the red wine vinegar and sugar and boil until the vinegar has evaporated and the sugar has caramelised. Reduce the cooking juices if necessary, then add the caramel to taste. Toss the cooked oxtail with the walnuts and pour the sauce back over the oxtail. Serve with mashed potato, polenta or pasta.

Serves 12, main course

catherine kerry

chef

adelaide

Catherine Kerry believes that there is something magical about olive oil. 'The transformation from the bitter, inhospitable, inedible fruit to unctuous oil is miraculous,' she says.

Catherine Kerry grew up in Algeria with her French mother and

English father, and olives were a part of both the North African and French food her family ate. Green olives went with chicken and mushrooms in the classic French style, while olives and preserved lemons went with chicken in the North African style.

Her family came to Australia when she was eleven and Catherine remembers going to the chemist with her mother to buy Faulding Olive Oil: 'I can still remember the flavour of that oil, and it was good. We didn't know about the Italian presses that existed in Adelaide at the time. Then we discovered the Star Grocery in Hindley Street. There were sacks of beans on the floor, and the shelves were stacked high with exotic produce. It was like going into another world. We bought our olive oil in flagons.

'My parents made me eccentric, and proud to be different. We never felt bad about being different in Australia. There was no way we would even put a piece of lettuce in our mouths without olive oil on it.' Catherine finds it a happy coincidence when something practical coincides with fashion. In this sense she likens olive oil to Doc Martens. Olive oil is versatile, rich and good for you and it is natural, nothing needs to be done to it.

Catherine has coined the phrase 'food miles'. The best food is that which has the shortest amount of travel (processing) between the source and the table. Olive oil doesn't have to travel far at all. She compares olive oil to wine, saying that it too is very romantic as you can taste the soil and life that went before the pressing: 'To appreciate olive oil it is not necessary to have a sophisticated palate. We must have the freedom for some of us to become obsessed by things. Others can simply enjoy them.'

In Catherine's family, olives were more than a canape or garnish. They were considered a vegetable in themselves. When she cooks, she knows the flavour she is aiming for from memory: 'I never serve my olives undressed.

I particularly like the tiny roadside olives. After preserving them, I dress them with olive oil and cumin or other herbs and spices. This is the Magreb influence.'

As far as olive oils go, at home Catherine has a posh one, a salad one and a can of an ordinary one. She says that if you want to use olive oil in Asian food, the world is not going to fall apart. Of course, if you want authentic Asian food it is best to use traditional oils: 'All over the world now we expect eclecticism. We're desperate to control so much knowledge these days. Did we get used to olive oil going with tomatoes and basil, or is there something intrinsic, something spiritual, about it?'

Catherine Kerry stands up for the use of oil and butter in cooking and criticises the denial and rituals of food fanatics. She points out that the body needs calories to operate and credits her clear complexion to both oil and butter in her diet: 'The population is becoming obsessed with health. For many people, health is the new religion and food is the new medicine. These new believers are very moralistic. Everything is either good or bad.'

And there certainly doesn't seem to be anything bad about the dishes Catherine describes – wood-fired curd drenched in olive oil, tomatoes with olive oil, and bouillabaisse finished off with olive oil to emulsify and give an unctuousness to the dish.

Catherine Kerry likes Australian olive oils. She believes that Australia has the right climate for both wine and olive oil production and is making interesting, good quality oils. She claims that Australians have lost their cultural cringe, and that anything Australian is fashionable at the moment. She wonders, however, whether oil producers will go the way of winemakers, standardising their oils and making them over-elegant.

Catherine uses imported oils to add more interest to her food. She thinks it is great that Australians can choose between Joe Grilli's fabulous oils and the expensive products imported from abroad. She uses both and changes her oils when her palate wants a shake up.

The first four of Cath's recipes are for marinated olives with a North African (Magreb) slant. They can be used for up to two days after being prepared but they are best when the dressing is still fresh.

500 g small black olives • zest of 2 lemons • ¹/₂ tspn paprika • ¹/₄ tspn ground cumin • ¹/₄ tspn ground chilli • 1 tbspn olive oil • pulp of the lemon, cut into small dice

Small black olives (nicoise) with paprika and cumin

Combine and allow to marinate for 2 to 3 hours before serving.

Kalamata olives with orange zest

500 g kalamata olives • 4 tspn chopped oregano (or 2 tspn crumbled dried oregano) • 1 tspn fresh rosemary, chopped • 2 tspn fresh thyme leaves • zest of 1 orange • 1 tbspn olive oil

Combine and marinate for 2 to 3 hours before serving.

Semi-ripe 'purple' olives are those that are turning from green to mottled purple black. Black olives may also be used. 500 g purple olives • 1 clove garlic, chopped • 6 sprigs coriander and 1 sprig parsley, chopped together finely •

Purple olives with preserved lemons

1 tspn paprika • $^1/_2$ tspn ground cumin • 2 tbspn lemon juice •
1 tbspn olive oil • $^1/_4$ preserved lemon (see page 59), cut
into fine strips (discard the pulp of the lemon, and only
use the rind)

Combine and allow to marinate for 2 to 3 hours before serving.

Black olives with cumin and orange zest

500 g black olives • 2 strips orange peel, removed with a
zester • $^1/_2$ tspn coarsely ground cumin • $^1/_4$ tspn dried chilli
• olive oil to coat

Combine and allow to stand for a while before serving.

Anchoïade

This Provencale 'sauce' has a mayonnaise-like consistency.
You can add as much olive oil as the mixture will hold.
20 anchovy fillets, rinsed of salt if necessary • 8 to 10
cloves garlic • 1 tbspn red wine vinegar • up to 250 ml olive
oil • small handful parsley, finely chopped • slices of
baguette, toasted (or crudites, especially celery)

In a food processor, chop together anchovies and garlic. Add the vinegar
then the oil in a slow drizzle (drop by drop to begin) as for mayonnaise.
Add the parsley and process until just chopped. Adjust the seasoning
with a little more black pepper and more vinegar if necessary. Spread on
toasted bread, place under the griller for a few seconds if desired.
Anchoïade can also be served in a bowl as a dip with raw vegetables.

Olive and parsley salad

1 lemon • 1 cup kalamata olives • 1 large bunch flat parsley •
1 garlic clove, finely chopped (optional) • 1 tbspn well

flavoured olive oil • salt and freshly ground black pepper
to taste

Take the zest from the lemon and set aside. Peel the lemon so that no white pith remains and cut into small cubes, reserving any juice. Pull the leaves from the parsley. Stone the olives and cut into strips. Mix all ingredients together and serve.

Salad of oranges, onion and olives

3 large oranges • 1 red onion, finely sliced • black olives as
required • trickle of rosewater and olive oil

Trim oranges of their peel and pith, then slice. Make a salad with oranges, onions, and dressing. Pit the olives (never buy ready pitted ones). Scatter over the top.

North african eggplant salad

6 medium eggplants • salt as required • oil for frying
(with a clove of garlic optional)
dressing: 1 clove garlic, finely chopped • 2 tbspn olive oil •
2 tbspn lemon juice • $^1/_2$ tspn pepper • $^1/_2$ tspn paprika •
$^1/_2$ tspn chilli flakes • 1 tbspn flat parsley, chopped •
1 tbspn coriander, finely chopped • 18 black olives

Slice off a little of the eggplant skin in vertical lines. Slice or halve the eggplant, depending on size. Salt the slices and allow to drain in a colander. Rinse and squeeze out excess water. In fairly hot oil, fry slices until golden. Drain. Arrange slices on a serving dish and pour over dressing. Top with chopped parsley, coriander and olives.

Caponata

1 kg eggplant, cut into cubes and salted • olive oil for frying • 2 onions • 5 stalks celery, cut into cubes • 1 tbspn sugar • 4 tbspn red wine vinegar • 2 tbspn tomato paste • 25 g (4 squares) dark chocolate • 175 g green olives, pitted and chopped • 2 tspn capers, rinsed of salt • chopped parsley and toasted almonds for garnish

Rinse and drain eggplant. Squeeze dry and fry in olive oil until golden. Set aside. Tip off most of the oil and cook the onions and celery until soft. Add the eggplant. Make the sauce in a pan by heating together the sugar, vinegar, tomato and finally the chocolate. Stir in the olives and pour the sauce over the vegetables. Garnish.

Chermoula

This Tunisian marinade is wonderful for meat, especially lamb, and fish.

For 1.5 kg of fish fillets from a large firm fish such as snapper, snook or trevally:

3 large cloves garlic, ground with 2 tspn salt • 2 tbspn ground cumin • 2 tbspn paprika • $1/4$ to 1 full tspn chilli flakes • 4 tbspn flat parsley and coriander, chopped • 2 tbspn olive oil • 2 tbspn lemon juice

Mix all the ingredients together and rub the mixture on fish (or meat). Allow to sit for at least an hour (longer for meat) before grilling. Alternatively, once marinated, place portions of fish covered in chermoula in aluminium foil and bake in the oven or kettle barbecue.

8 serving portions of chicken on the bone (both breast and leg) • $^1/_2$ tspn powdered ginger • $^1/_2$ tspn black pepper • $^1/_2$ tspn saffron, soaked in 1 tbspn water • $^1/_2$ tspn ground cumin • $^1/_2$ tspn sweet paprika • 1 generous tbspn chopped parsley • 1 generous tbspn chopped coriander • 2 cloves garlic, finely chopped • 1 large onion, finely chopped • salt to taste • 900 g green olives, preferably cracked greek olives • $^1/_2$ cup fresh lemon juice • 1 preserved lemon, skin only, finely sliced

Chicken with mountains of olives

Place the chicken in a large casserole with all the ingredients except the olives and lemon. Cover with water and bring to the boil. Reduce heat and simmer for 30 minutes. Meanwhile, stone the olives using a paring knife or by cracking each one with a hammer and removing the stone. If the olives are very bitter, cover them with water, bring to the boil and cook for 5 minutes. Repeat twice if necessary. Add olives to the chicken with the lemon juice. Continue cooking until the chicken is very tender. Remove the chicken to a shallow, oven-proof serving dish and brown in a hot oven. Reduce the liquid in the casserole to a thick gravy and adjust the seasoning. Add the pickled lemon. To serve, cover the chicken with the sauce and olives.

Serves 6–8, main course

6 duck legs • 4 tbspn salt • 4 tbspn sugar • 3 cloves garlic • 1 tspn fennel seeds • 1 tspn cumin seeds • 1 cup good green olives • 4 quarters preserved lemon (see page 59) • 1 brown onion • 1 cup white wine • knob of butter

Cured duck legs with olives and preserved lemons

'Cure' the legs the day before cooking. To do this, grind the spices in a clean coffee grinder, leaving a little texture. Mash or chop the garlic with a little salt. Mix together the spices, garlic, sugar and salt. Trim the duck legs of excess fat and place, flesh side up, in a bowl, covered with the spice mixture. Allow to sit in the refrigerator for at least 24 hours.

Roast the duck legs in a moderate oven (180°C) for about 30 minutes, or until they are browned, tender and the flesh has pulled away from the drumstick bone. Reserve the duck fat and juices. Keep the duck legs warm while preparing the sauce.

To make the sauce: remove the flesh from the lemons and discard. Slice the lemon into match sticks. Remove the stones from the olives by hitting each one smartly with a hammer or handle of a kitchen knife. The olive will split and the stone will come away easily. Halve the olives. Halve and slice the onion, then soften in 2 tablespoons of duck fat. Add the olives to the onions. Cook them a little, then add the wine and as much duck juice as can be salvaged from the bottom of the duck fat. Bring the sauce to the boil and, watching that it does not boil over, reduce the liquid by half. Add the butter to finish the sauce. Add the lemon at the end just to heat it.

Serve the duck with the sauce poured over, preferably on a bed of small green lentils cooked with onion, duck fat, a little tomato paste and a touch of cumin.

Serves 6, main course

Lamb back straps are ideal for this recipe. They are easy to cook and have little waste.

North african-style marinade for lamb

For each kilo of meat:

125 to 250 ml cup olive oil • 1 tspn coarse, freshly ground black pepper • 1$^{1}/_{2}$ tspn cumin (preferably freshly ground) • 1 tspn ground cinnamon • $^{1}/_{2}$ tspn allspice • 2 cloves garlic, crushed with the back of a knife

Mix together all marinade ingredients. Layer the lamb in a shallow dish, spreading the marinade over each layer. Cover with plastic wrap and store in the refrigerator for at least 24 hours. Cook on a hot barbecue, turning once. Be careful not to overcook the meat and allow it to rest for at least 10 minutes before serving. The meat will continue to cook from its own heat once it is off the fire.

2 eggs • 200 g caster sugar • 80 ml olive oil • 100 ml white wine • 200 g self-raising flour

Gateau au vin blanc (cake with white wine)

Beat together, by hand or in a food processor, the eggs and sugar until they are pale. Gradually add the oil, then the white wine. Sift the flour, then add egg to the mixture. Fold in just enough to blend. Pour into a buttered and floured loaf tin and bake in a moderate oven (180°C) for about 30 minutes or until the cake is cooked. It should have risen enough to have split and be nicely golden. Cool in the tin on a rack for 5 minutes before unmoulding. Serve cold or just warm with thick cream and a favourite conserve.

Makroud

500 g pitted dates • 1 tbspn rosewater • 2 tspn cinnamon • 500 g semolina • 30 g caster sugar • 60 g butter • 1 egg • approximately 50 ml water • approximately 750 ml olive oil for frying • 300 g honey, thinned with a little water

In a blender, make a paste with the dates, rosewater and cinnamon. (For very dry dates you may have to heat them with a little water first.) In a bowl, make the pastry by rubbing the butter and oil into the semolina. Add egg and sugar and bind with just enough water. Halve the dough. Spread one half out to $^1/_2$ cm thickness. Spread over the dates and top with the rest of the semolina dough. Cut into diamonds or squares. Deep fry until golden in hot oil. Dip into thinned honey. These little cakes can be made in advance and kept in a covered container for several days.

Cuisse de dâmes (lady's thighs)

$^1/_2$ cup olive oil • $^1/_2$ cup white wine • $^1/_2$ cup caster sugar • 375 g self-raising flour (or 250 g self-raising flour, 125 g plain flour for a firmer texture) • $^1/_2$ tspn caraway seeds or $^1/_2$ tspn good vanilla essence

Beat together the olive oil, white wine and sugar until the sugar is dissolved. Add the flour and flavouring to make a soft dough. Knead until smooth. Cut dough into four pieces. Roll each piece out in a thin sausage and cut into finger shapes. Place on a baking sheet and bake in a moderate oven (180°C) until golden. When out of the oven, cool on a rack and dust with icing sugar if desired.

Chris Manfield thinks the modern response to olive oil is based on people's preoccupation with diet. People are obsessed about not eating butter and so have adopted the age old product of olive oil. She says that she too is maniacally obsessed with food: 'I'm a great lover of history and travel. I work out where things come from and the history of their flavour in a broad social context. Olive oil is so sensual. Imagine bathing in it. There is a lot of sexual innuendo attached to olive oil.'

Chris says that food culture reflects how advanced a country is: 'Australians have grown up an awful lot. Twenty years ago we were in the wilderness, Australian food was bland and pedestrian. There was no excitement or sensuality in cooking. We are now a lot more discerning in what we want.'

At Chris Manfield's Potts Point restaurant, they don't serve oil on the table unless it is requested. Chris admits that she is a butter freak, but she uses gallons of olive oil in her cooking: 'Olive oil is basically a Mediterranean cooking medium. Modern Australian cooks must look at traditions – before you can change something you have to understand it.'

Chris uses lots of spices and aromatic Asian ingredients and says that these generally don't go with olive oil. But she also loves the food of North Africa and the Mediterranean. She dries her own tomatoes and uses olive oil with them, as with capsicums, capers, caper berries, pimentos, and some of the milder chillies: 'Some oils are very one dimensional; for example, peanut oil is only good for deep frying. Olive oil is rich and luscious, and it has many uses. It has a wonderful feel in the mouth. You don't feel like you're using sump oil. I use olive oil to enhance the flavour of certain foods. You don't use other oils that way.'

Chris likes a light oil for cooking. She always uses extra virgin for her salad dressings, and in her succulent duck salad, for example, she uses cabernet vinegar and Romanico oil with jelly from the duck. Chris uses virgin oil for anything eaten at room temperature. She is also fond of garnishing dishes with a lighter olive oil mixed with diced preserved lemon.

Olives also make an appearance in Chris's cooking. She advises cooks to consider the salt content of olives because it will affect the dish they are used in. Whenever Chris uses preserved lemons, she uses olives, usually black but sometimes green. When she thinks of octopus, she thinks of black olives, sun-dried tomatoes and garlic: 'One ingredient should never overpower other flavours in a dish. Strong oils should be balanced with other ingredients so you get a reaction happening in your mouth. When people are tasting and choosing olive oils, they should be more confident of their own tastes and using their own palate. Like wine, oil is very personal and subjective. You can't have hard and fast rules about which oil is good and which isn't.'

chris manfield's
recipes

Roasted garlic aïoli 1 head of garlic • 2 pinches of sea salt • 25 ml lemon juice, strained • 25 ml white wine vinegar • 3 pinches of freshly ground white pepper • 2 egg yolks • 250 ml virgin olive oil • 250 ml vegetable oil

Preheat oven to 180°C and wrap the head of garlic in foil. Bake the garlic for 30 minutes or until soft. Squeeze out the soft garlic cloves and mix with the salt in a mortar and pestle. Blend the garlic and salt in a food processor with the lemon juice, vinegar, pepper and egg yolks until well incorporated. With the motor running, slowly drizzle in the combined oils in a thin, steady stream until incorporated and the mayonnaise becomes thick. To store, spoon the mayonnaise into a container, seal and refrigerate.

Grilled rare tuna steak with fennel, green garlic and roasted garlic aïoli

6 x 150 g trimmed tuna steaks (2 cm thick) • 100 ml olive oil • 2 small bulbs fennel, finely sliced • 3 green garlic stems, finely sliced • 5 cocktail onions, caramelised and cut into quarters • 25 ml lemon juice, strained • 50 ml virgin olive oil • pinch sea salt • pinch freshly ground white pepper • 3 tspn chopped green fennel tops • 6 tblspn roasted garlic aïoli (see recipe above)

Preheat a char grill pan or barbecue. Brush the tuna steaks with half the olive oil and set aside. Heat a frying pan, add the remaining olive oil and gently sauté the fennel and green garlic until just softened. Add the caramelised onion and warm through. Transfer the vegetables to a bowl. Make a vinaigrette by mixing lemon juice and virgin olive oil with salt and pepper. Stir the vinaigrette into the fennel mixture with the fennel tops, then spoon the vegetables onto serving plates. Quickly sear the tuna steaks on the hot grill for 1 minute on each side – just enough to seal and colour the surface, leaving the inside very rare and pink but warmed through. Put the fish on the sautéed fennel and garlic and spoon over some aïoli. Serve immediately.

Serves 6, main course

ian parmenter

chef

fremantle

Ian describes himself humbly as a domestic cook – 'a keen amateur with forty years cooking experience'. He has cooked only twice in restaurants, and that is as much as he intends to do.

Ian's ABC television show is broadcast in fifteen countries. In 1996 it won the Prix de la Professions (the Presenters' Award) at the Festival de la Télé Gourmande in France: 'The first thing I think about when I wake up is food. While I'm coming to, I think about what I will cook that evening. I'm food centric, my world revolves around the plate. I think you're born with it or it comes from the first few years of your life. I grew up in England for nine years without any decent food. It was only in Belgium that I came across good food, and there it was mostly butter. The only place you could buy olive oil when I grew up was at the chemist. I started using olive oil in England when I was in my mid twenties. Australia is probably ahead of England in per capita consumption of olive oil. My mother still doesn't have olive oil in her kitchen.'

Ian pushed olive oil as a substitute for animal fats even before he became involved with the International Olive Oil Council. He recommends a Mediterranean diet rather than a traditional European one. It is unfortunate, he says, that fatty acids such as margarine are being promoted with the same fervour as olive oil: 'The way we live is insane. Mediterranean people would never wander around a shopping centre at lunch time with a bucket of chips and a diet coke in each hand. I don't care how busy I am, I always stop for lunch. People should play with their food until they find what they like. Palates have to be very sophisticated to understand the nuance of olive oil flavour. My most exciting experience with olive oil was when I stayed in a hotel in Provence. The ancient

Romans had used the site to produce olive oil at the aqueduct. In the stone floored dining room there were wooden shafts and wheels that were beautifully preserved because they had been used for oil production for so long. I hope olive oil will preserve me as well.'

Ian tries new oils all the time. Extra virgin for salads and shallow pan frying, extra light, canola or peanut oil for deep frying. He reminds cooks that food that is deep fried absorbs less oil than food that is shallow fried. The best way to test this is with a slice of eggplant.

Ian believes that people are starting to understand that some foods will taste better if they are prepared using extra virgin olive oil: 'Taste is what it boils down to in the end. Taste can vary like wine; many oils have a flat, consistent flavour. But with olive oil, you can explore the different taste of olives.'

Ian does not confine his use of olive oil to Mediterranean food. He points out that Elizabeth David's recipe for Chicken Provencale uses butter, but that he uses olive oil for those sorts of dishes. He uses olive oil in many sweet pastries, because it reduces the saturated fat in the dish. But he wouldn't use olive oil in a baklava because the flavour of the oil still comes through.

Ten years ago Ian would have had a bottle of olive oil in the pantry for three or four months. Now he goes through a bottle every couple of weeks.

Ian Parmenter thinks that Australian oils stand up well against European oils: 'But there is olive oil snobbism. Olive oil flavour varies so much according to *terroir*. Anything as interesting as the grape or the olive will be discussed at length, and people will always be adding to the vocabulary. In Australia different regions are producing different flavours. Another part of the mystique stems from the packaging. If the oils are presented in bottles that are a couple of metres high, people think that it must be very special.'

He says that Australians will develop a bible for the olive oil industry, because there is a huge demand and it will keep going: 'What Australia needs to look at is import replacement rather than becoming an exporting country.'

ian parmenter's
recipes

Greek octopus

3 large octopus legs (about 1 kg - make sure they are tenderised before buying) • 250 ml extra virgin olive oil • 1 cup lemon juice • 1 tbspn chopped fresh oregano (or 1 tspn dried) • 1 tspn cracked black pepper

Mix marinade ingredients. Marinate octopus legs for 1 hour in two-thirds of the marinade mixture, no longer. Use a glass or stainless bowl, or one which will not react with the acid in the lemon juice. Coil each leg on a barbecue plate, starting with the thick ending and finishing with the thin. Barbecue for 3 to 4 minutes each side or until the suckers become white. Cut into bite-sized pieces and toss with remaining marinade.
Serves 6, main course

Olive focaccia

250 g plain white flour • 250 g wholemeal flour (additional plain flour for kneading) • 17 g sachet dried yeast • 1 tspn sugar • 1 teaspoon salt (optional) • 2 tablespoons olive oil • 1 medium onion finely chopped • 2 tablespoons black olives, stoned and chopped • 2 tablespoons fresh herbs (preferably rosemary, parsley, oregano and thyme or 1 tablespoon mixed

dried herbs), additional olives for final stage (these may be left un-stoned)

Mix 1 tablespoon flour, the sugar and yeast with a couple of tablespoons of tepid water and allow to stand for 20 minutes. This will activate the yeast.

In a large bowl mix flour, 1 tablespoon olive oil and salt. Add yeast mixture and mix well. Cover bowl with damp tea towel and leave in a warm place for one hour.

Meanwhile, put remaining oil in frying pan and over medium heat cook onion until it has softened (about 5 minutes). Stir in chopped olives and herbs and cook briefly (about 30 seconds), set aside.

Remove the dough to a floured work bench and knead for 5 to 6 minutes. Knead in olive-herb mixture.

Divide in two, flatten each into a flat pizza shape, put on oiled pizza tin or baking tray, cover with a damp tea-towel and leave in a warm place for an hour.

Before baking, dimple surface of each loaf with fingers, spread a little more olive oil, dot olives around. Sprinkle on a little sea salt.

Bake in a moderately hot oven 200°C for about 25 minutes, or until top is golden brown and bottom is light brown.

Makes 2 loaves

ann oliver

chef

adelaide

Ann Oliver admits that she didn't cook anything until she was twenty, saying that she could barely make a decent cup of coffee. A group of Austrian friends shamed her into cooking and, after six months in Austria, cooking became her passion. In 1981 she started the legendary Mistress Augustine's restaurant in Adelaide. She had no previous restaurant experience but learnt by watching Phillip Searle who owned Possums next door.

Ann has been preserving her own olives for fifteen years and now has a tried and true method. She remembers, however, that some of her early experiments were not only expensive but fraught with mishaps. She was told that in Cyprus, green olives were put unsplit into brine for two weeks then into extra virgin olive oil with coriander, garlic and chillies. Two hundred dollars later she had forty litres of enormous green olives, which she tasted each week in the hope that they were becoming less bitter. After eighteen months she threw the whole experiment in the bin, with the exception of a two litre bucket. She tried some of the olives a year later and they were brilliant.

The markets at Pooraka where Ann bought her olives put her in contact with centuries of culinary experience. She learnt from the growers that they used to hang olives in hessian bags from trees to preserve them. Ann then devised her own preservation method with chicken crates and rock salt. She leaves her olives for two to four weeks until they are no longer bitter.

Ann remembers the good days when she and Jane Ferrari did an olive tasting for David Jones. They were allowed to open every bottle in the store, which gave her an overview of oils from around the world. At the tasting, which was open to the public, they planted a rancid oil and people picked it as being off. Ann believes that tastings are important because every culture prefers its own olive oil. They like what they are used to, not products that are better or worse.

Ann Oliver's European friends take her to task because she uses extra virgin oil for everything. They say it isn't right, that she should use an everyday oil and keep her special oil for salads.

Olive oil is used in a French way in Ann's kitchen. She loves the combination of oil and butter, particularly for sautéing meat.

Ann says that the combination for marinating preserved olives are endless. She suggests doing green olives with coriander, garlic and chilli in olive oil and leaving them for two weeks. Or marinating black olives in olive oil, lots of garlic, lavender and orange rind for the true taste of Provence. One of Ann's favourite hors d'oeuvres is stuffed, crumbed and deep fried olives served with aïoli. The olives can also be stuffed with a porcini mushroom risotto or with a meat farce with plenty of pine nuts and herbs.

When Ann visited Greece during a recent vintage, she saw the Greek people suffering because world demand for olive oil had tripled in the last six years. Increased consumption and demand had pushed the price of olive oil well beyond the reach of many of its traditional consumers. Greeks hold a special place in their hearts for olive oil, but even they are looking for alternatives. Ann believes that this will happen in Australia as well, because people won't pay the price. She thinks that oils such as maize oil, corn oil, and 'ghastly' canola oil, which is bleached to get the red out, will become popular again.

Ann acknowledges that very often people's choices are based on economics rather than on health or flavour. But, for all that, she thinks that people are learning and that there are now many who can tell the difference between great olive oil and poor quality olive oil.

According to Ann, people get excited about olive oil because, like a new perfume, it is the subject of an intensive marketing exercise. She claims that in the 1980s Americans didn't know the difference between olive oil and canola oil, and that they still have limited knowledge compared to Australians: 'Australian chefs started using olive oil in the 1980s. If someone had a salad in your restaurant and said, "Wow, that's beautiful," you would reply, "It's beautiful because of the olive oil." That was the way it was introduced to the public. Olive oil has now become entrenched in every day life.' I knew Australia had come a long way with olive oil when a friend's husband, originally from Genoa and a great one for pooh poohing Australian oils, tasted a salad made with Joseph Foothills and declared, Yes!'

ann oliver's
recipes

Mediterranean whole baked fish

6 lemons • extra virgin olive oil as required • 10 cm sprig rosemary • 500 ml black olives • sea salt and freshly ground black pepper to taste • 6 whole fish (approximately 350 g) or 1 whole fish (approximately 2.5 kg)

Cut one and a half lemons into wedges, trim them, remove any seeds, wrap them in a damp cloth and refrigerate. Zest the rest of the lemons, juice them and strain the juice into a measuring jug. Add three times the volume of lemon juice in olive oil and whisk together. Diamond score the fish on both sides and brush the lemon juice and olive oil onto both sides of the fish, including the head, until it is used up. Leaf the rosemary and scatter the leaves and the olives over the fish. Season lightly with salt and generously with pepper. Cook the fish in a baking dish lined with baking paper in a 200°C oven for 15 to 20 minutes for the small fish and approximately 45 minutes for the large. Carefully transfer to a serving plate, drizzle a little extra oil over the fish and garnish with the prepared lemon wedges and zest. Serve hot or at room temperature with rocket salad and grilled polenta.

If there is any left over fish, mash it with some chopped pitted black olives, anchovies and capers, and mix into a lemony mayonnaise. This is delicious spread on thick dry toast. Make the mayonnaise by mixing or processing one cold extra large egg, two pinches of sea salt, a little freshly ground black pepper, 20 g of smooth French mustard, and 250 ml of cold olive oil. Process until thick, then work in 50 ml of cold strained lemon juice and the grated rind of half a lemon.

Serves 6, main course

Pasta with black olives, chilli, garlic, cracked pepper and parsley

2 small hot chillies • 6 large cloves garlic • 300 g good black olives, pitted • 15 g whole black pepper, coarsely and freshly cracked • 1 bunch of flat leafed parsley • 40 ml joseph foothills extra virgin olive oil • regianno parmesan, finely shaved

Mix everything together in a stainless steel bowl and stand it over the hot water in which the pasta is cooking. Drain the cooked pasta well, tip into the bowl, toss through the ingredients and serve with the parmesan.

Serves 6, first course

Grilled fillet of kangaroo with black olive glaze and black olive and goat's cheese bread

bread: 15 g yeast • 15 g caster sugar • 15 g salt • 395 g strong flour (and a little extra for the board) • 275 ml milk • 150 g black olives, pitted • 250 g soft curd goat's cheese • olive oil for brushing tins
kangaroo: 6 thick fillets of kangaroo between 175 g and 200 g each • 100 ml joseph olive oil • 250 g kalamata black olives, pitted • 100 ml red wine • 50 ml balsamic vinegar • 300 ml veal glaze (available from provedores)

To make the bread: warm the milk to blood temperature in the microwave oven – if the milk is cold, 45 seconds on high in a microwave should be sufficient. Place the sugar and yeast into a bowl and whisk until the mixture starts to go runny. Add sufficient milk and flour to form a batter of crepe consistency. Set to one side until the mixture bubbles. Mix in the remaining flour and milk, knead the dough for a few minutes, then mix in the salt and olives. Knead half the goat's cheese into the dough, then add the remaining cheese, trying to leave it slightly lumpy in texture. Brush the mixing bowl with olive oil, and turn the dough into the bowl. Cover with plastic food wrap and allow to rise until at least doubled in volume. Lightly flour the bench top, punch the dough down, and turn it out onto the bench. Knead the dough again, then, using a knife, divide the dough into twelve equal portions. Put these into small greased tins, or keep as one loaf on a greased oven tray. Allow the bread to rise again. Preheat oven to 200°C. Cook the bread until browned and crusty on top. Turn off the oven, leaving the door open to cool the oven a little, then turn the bread out onto a rack.

If the olives for the sauce have been in oil, gently rinse them under cold running water. Place the olive oil into a bowl. Remove any sinew from the kangaroo, then roll the fillets through the olive oil. Put the wine and vinegar into a saucepan and place it on high heat. Reduce the liquids by half, then remove them from the heat. Add the glaze and olives to the saucepan, and return to a very gentle heat, shaking the pan occasionally until the glaze is melted, then remove from heat. Heat oven to 100°C. Place a resting tray and rack, and bread and dinner plates in the oven. Put the grill pan on the highest heat and, when hot, quickly sear the kangaroo fillets, placing them in the resting oven as they are finished. Rest for approximately 10 minutes for rare to medium-rare meat.

To serve: mop any blood from the fillets, then place one on each plate. Divide the sauce between the plates, spooning it over the top of the kangaroo. Place a loaf on each plate, putting the remaining loaves on a plate to put on the table. Some steamed and buttered asparagus and new potatoes are excellent with this dish.

Serves 6, main course

'Chile new mexico' filled with walnuts, green olives and pork

packet dried 'chile new mexico' (available from David Jones and good delicatessens. approximately 84 g to 110 g - about 10 chillies) • 250 g walnuts • 200 g brown onions (1 large), peeled and finely chopped • 3 cloves of garlic, peeled and mascerated • 75 g lard or rendered fat from speck • 5 g sea salt • generous amount of freshly ground white pepper • 250 g tub of your favourite green olives • 5 g ground cinnamon • pinch ground cloves • 1 small bunch coriander • 3 sprigs mint • zest from 1 orange, very finely chopped • 500 g lean pork or beef mince • 1 extra large egg (61 g) • 250 ml milk • 150 g plain flour • approximately 150 g dried fine bread crumbs • oil for deep frying • 6 limes

The night before serving, put chillies into a bowl and cover them with cold water. Before going to bed make sure they are submerged in the water. Use a plate and weight if necessary.

Preheat oven to 150°C. Put the walnuts onto a tray and dry roast them until they are lightly coloured. Allow to cool completely. Put the lard in a heavy-based pan and place it on medium heat. Add the onion, garlic, salt, pepper, cinnamon and cloves and sauté until golden. Scrape into the food processor and allow to become completely cold before proceeding. Wash the coriander and mint, dry it off as much as possible, chop it roughly and add the orange rind to the onion mixture, then stir through the olives and walnuts. Chop roughly on pulse, then mix thoroughly into the meat by hand. Put the mixture into a large piping bag fitted with a 1 centimetre round nozzle. Carefully tip the chillies into a colander. Allow them to drain for a few minutes, then dry them gently on a paper towel. Make a slit just large enough to fit the nozzle into the tip of each chilli. Holding a chilli carefully in your hand, fill it with a share of the filling and return it to the paper towel.

Put the egg into a bowl, add a little salt and pepper, and whisk thoroughly. Whisk in the milk. Put the flour into another bowl, then crumb the chillies in the normal manner of flour, egg wash and bread crumbs. Store for up to 2 hours on paper towel uncovered in the fridge.

Preheat the deep fryer to 160°C. Deep fry the stuffed chillies three at a time, draining them well on paper towel. Cut limes into wedges. Arrange the chillies decoratively in a serving bowl with the lime wedges scattered about them. Serve at room temperature or just warm, with a tangy lime and avocado mayonnaise or with aïoli. A combination of the two would be perfect.

Serves 6, first course

Olive's glacé olives   black olives • 20 g sea salt per litre of water • 1 kg caster sugar per kg olives

Prick black olives several times with a sterilised needle and soak in a saline solution of 20 grams of sea salt for every litre of water for 1 week. Rinse them well under cold running water, then put them into a large stainless steel or enamel saucepan. For every kilo of olives, add 1 kilo of caster sugar. Simmer for 1 minute and remove from the heat. Bring the olives to the boil and immediately remove them from the heat twice a day until the syrup is thick and purple and the olive has a translucent glaced appearance and a sweet, almost date-like, taste – 7 to 10 days approximately.

zeffie kathreptis and lew kathreptis

The Kathreptis family are known throughout Australia for their culinary expertise, warmth and charm. Olives and olive oil have always been part of their lives.

Zeffie was born in Australia in 1929 to Greek and Turkish parents. She can remember her mother not being able to get enough olive oil and having to cook their chips in dripping. She used to send the kids to the old Adelaide Gaol and to North Terrace to pick olives that she would use for pickling.

By the time Zeffie's children – Irene, Lew and Anthony – were born, olive oil was readily available. The Star Grocery sold imported olive oil and vendors would sell olive oil in the streets off carts containing produce from Port Pirie and Renmark. Emmanuel Giakoumis made oil in Edwardstown in the late 1950s. He would sell it in eighteen-litre tins. When Zeffie's children had grown up they used to buy a tin and share it around as it was too much for one couple.

Food has always been a family concern for the Kathreptises. Lew and Zeffie ran the kitchen at Mezes in Adelaide, while Irene looked after front of house.

Lew later worked in London as the chef-in-residence for Dr Neal Blewett, Australia's High Commissioner in London. He then travelled through Spain and Morocco before settling in Sydney.

A truly accomplished chef, Lew is not only seduced by the flavour of olive oil, but also by the colour. He loves the golden glow from the bottle and believes that people are subconsciously drawn to the colour.

Zeffie Kathreptis used to blend her olive oil with a vegetable oil when she first opened Mezes restaurant because straight olive oil was then too strong for the Australian palate.

At home Zeffie normally uses a cheaper oil for frying. She says that you can tell if an oil is off when you start to heat it. If her oil gets too hot, she simply adds some cold oil. She uses olive oil in pastries, salads, sauces, marinades and sometimes for frying.

Zeffie also uses olive oil cosmetically. When her skin is dry she rubs herself with it. She doesn't use it in her hair because it is hard to wash out. Her family also believes in olive oil's ability to ward off the evil eye.

Lew Kathreptis loves the variety of olive oils. He says that versatility in an oil is important. He has about ten different olive oils in his kitchen at home. Lew stresses that cooks need to understand how to use olive oil properly. He uses heavy oils for fish and light oils for salad. He uses olive oil to make all his mayonnaise, but the type of oil depends on what the mayonnaise is to go with. For a roasted garlic mayonnaise he uses a lighter oil so that the garlic flavour can come through. Lew likes a lighter oil with sweetbreads and cured meats, and heavy gutsy oils with blanched vegetables. He suggests using peppery oils with raw meat (carpaccio). Lew points out that there are similarities between the Australian olive industry and the Australian cheese-making industry. Cheese and olives have been produced for centuries in the Mediterranean, and Australians have only just begun to experiment. Lew believes that Australians are delightfully naive when it comes to olive oil, and that there is still a novelty factor with it.

Lew recommends that Australians should not be in such a hurry to produce the right oils, as they will make mistakes along the way. He thinks that Australian olive oil producers should look to the Mediterranean for guidance.

Grilled swordfish with olive sauce and zucchini

fish: 6 x 200 g swordfish steaks • 200 ml olive oil • 250 ml white wine • 1 bay leaf, torn into pieces • 1 medium onion, thinly sliced • 1 tspn salt • 1 tspn white peppercorns

sauce: 1 large potato • 1 cup pitted and finely chopped green spanish olives • 120 ml extra virgin olive oil • 3 anchovy fillets, finely chopped • 1 tspn saffron • 2 tbspn oregano, finely chopped • $1/2$ tspn black peppercorns, coarsely ground • 2 small hot chillies, seeded and cut into julienne • grated zest of one orange • 2 tbspn roasted pinenuts • 2 tbspn raisins

zucchini: 6 small zucchini • 175 ml olive oil • 1 large onion, diced • 4 cloves garlic, minced • 3 tbspn white wine vinegar • 2 tspn sugar • salt and pepper to taste

To make the marinade: combine the olive oil, white wine, bayleaf, onion, salt, and peppercorns. Mix thoroughly. Immerse swordfish steaks in the marinade and allow to stand for a couple of hours, turning the steaks occasionally.

To make the sauce: grate the potato into a bowl and cover with 1 cup of water. Allow to stand for 2 hours. Drain and reserve 120 ml of the potato water and the sediment that is left in the bottom of the bowl, discard the potato. In a tablespoon toast the saffron over a low flame and dissolve in the reserved potato water. Allow it to infuse for at least 5 minutes. Combine all the other sauce ingredients with 2 teaspoons of the potato sediment. Cover and allow to stand for at least an hour so the flavours can develop.

To prepare the zucchinni: thinly slice the zucchini lengthwise. Place the slices in a colander and sprinkle with salt. Allow to drain for at least 30 minutes. Wash off the excess salt and pat the slices dry. Heat the olive oil in a wide frypan. Fry the zucchini in the oil until it is just turning colour, remove and drain on absorbent paper. Remove the zucchini from the paper and place in a deep dish. In the same oil, cook the onion until soft and translucent but not browned. Add the garlic and the sugar and cook for a few more moments. Add the vinegar and simmer for 5 minutes. Season with salt and pepper. Pour the onion mixture over the fried zucchini and marinate for a couple of hours.

To assemble the dish: heat the grill which will cook the swordfish steaks. Remove the steaks from the marinade and anything that adheres to them. Strain the marinade and reserve. Cook the steaks for 4 minutes on one side. Baste the fish with the reserved marinade and flip over and cook for another 4 minutes and baste once more. Meanwhile, drain the zucchini and divide onto warm serving plates. Place the cooked swordfish on top of each mound of zucchini. Give the sauce another good mix and sauce each steak. Serve immediately.

Serves 6, main course

Olive pies

filling: 60 ml olive oil • 500 g ligurian olives • 2 spanish onions, diced • 100 g pancetta, diced • 1 leek, diced • 2 ribs celery, diced • 100 g pine nuts, roasted • 100 g raisins • 4 bird's eye chillies, seeded and minced • 1/2 cup mint, chopped • $^1/_2$ cup parsley, chopped • grated zest of one lemon

pastry: 1 kg flour • 60 g fresh yeast • 5 g sugar • 10 g salt •

500 ml tepid water • 75 ml lemon juice • 150 ml olive oil •

sesame seeds for sprinkling

The day before making the pies, soak the olives in cold water, changing the water once or twice, to remove some of the salt content of the olives. The day of making the pies, drain the olives and pat dry. Pit the olives.

To make the filling: sauté the onions, pancetta, leek, and celery in the olive oil until almost caramelised. Add the olives to the remaining ingredients and remove from heat.

To make the pastry: dissolve the yeast in half a cup of the water and stir in the sugar. Add enough of the flour to create the consistency of thick cream. Allow to stand for a few minutes until it doubles in size. Dissolve the salt in the remainder of the water. Sift the remaining flour into a mixing bowl. Make a well in the centre and pour in the yeast mixture, the olive oil, the lemon juice and the salted water. Mix by hand until it amalgamates, then turn onto a lightly floured surface. Knead the pastry for 8 minutes. Clean the mixing bowl, oil it, then return the pastry to the bowl. Rotate the pastry in the oil to coat the surface. Cover the bowl with a clean tea towel and allow the pastry to double in volume.

Preheat the oven to 200°C. Oil a baking sheet. Knock down the pastry once it has risen and divide into 20 pieces of equal weight. Roll out each piece of pastry into a disc approximately 10 cm in diameter. Place a couple of tablespoons of the olive mixture in the centre of each disc. Brush the edges with water and fold in half to make crescent shapes. Seal the pies by pinching the edges together. Place on the oiled baking sheet. Brush each pie with water and sprinkle with sesame seeds. Loosely cover the pies with a clean tea towel and allow to stand for 5 minutes. Remove the towel and place the sheet of pies in the oven. Cook for 25 to 30 minutes, or until golden. Remove the pies from the baking sheet and place them on a rack to cool.

Makes 20

zeffie kathreptis's
recipes

Ripe black olives

Wash olives well and cut three slits in each. Put into water and soak for three days, changing water each day. To make brine, warm water with enough salt so that when an egg is immersed into the brine, an area of about a 10 cents coin breaks the surface (approximately 100 grams for every litre). Bring brine to the boil and cool. Put olives into sterilised glass jars. In each jar put 2 garlic cloves, a 6 centimetre stick of celery, including the leaves, 2 slices of lemon, a sprig of oregano (optional), small pieces of red capsicum, and the olives. Pour cooked brine into jars until three-quarters full. Pour vinegar to remaining volume, leaving enough room for a demitasse cup of olive oil. Place a small plate on top to keep olives submerged if necessary. The olives are ready when the bitterness has gone in approximately 10 weeks.

Walnut cake with olive oil

500 g self-raising flour • $^1/_2$ cup sultanas or raisins • 250 ml olive oil • 375 g sugar • 500 ml water • 125 ml brandy • 1 dstspn lemon rind • 1 tspn nutmeg • $1^1/_2$ cups finely chopped walnuts • 2 tspn cinnamon

Sift flour and spices. Wash and wipe sultanas or raisins and sift a little flour over them. Beat oil, add sugar, water, brandy, lemon peel. Fold in flour, nutmeg, walnuts and sultanas. Oil cake tin well, add mixture and bake in moderate oven for 1 hour. When cool, dust with icing sugar and extra cinnamon.

dough: 250 g unsalted butter • $^3/_4$ cup caster sugar • $^3/_4$ cup   **Finikia**
olive oil • $^3/_4$ cup orange juice • grated rind 1 orange •
6 cups self-raising flour
filling: 1 cup freshly chopped walnuts or mixed nuts •
$1^1/_2$ tspn cinnamon • pinch ground cloves • 1 tbspn sugar •
1 tbspn toasted sesame seeds • 1 tbspn toasted desiccated
coconut • 1 tbspn honey, thinned out with 2 tspn orange juice
syrup: 2 cups water • $1^1/_2$ cups sugar • $^1/_2$ cup honey • cinnamon
stick • lemon peel
topping: as for filling minus the honey and orange juice

Combine all the filling ingredients.

To make the dough: cream butter, sugar and orange rind until light and fluffy. Drizzle oil into creamed mixture while continuing beating. Stir in sifted flour, alternating with juice. Knead dough lightly for 1 minute.

Take 1 tablespoon of dough and flatten a little. Put teaspoon of filling into centre of dough and fold over to enclose the filling. Shape into an oval, pinching the ends to a point. Lightly grease a baking tray and bake in a moderate oven for 25 minutes. Cool.

Mix together all the topping ingredients. Place all the syrup ingredients in a heavy-based saucepan and stir over heat until sugar dissolves. Bring to boil and reduce heat to a gentle simmer for 10 minutes. Dip cooled biscuits into hot syrup. Leave for about 10 to 15 seconds. Sprinkle each biscuit with topping.

Every chef has his or her own opinion about the merits of using the finest extra virgin olive olive oil for cooking chips. Some believe it is an extravagant waste, others think that the better the oil used, the better the chip will be. Elizabeth David wrote in the 1950s that if olive oil is heated over 90°C, it loses its flavour. But, as Stephanie Alexander points out, this doesn't mean that it doesn't have other properties.

Zeffie Kathreptis says that when she uses a good olive oil for chips, they are sensational. Maggie Beer, however, uses cheaper oils when she raises the temperature in her cooking, because some of the flavour is lost. Chris Manfield agrees that olive oil produces a better flavour when it is used at room temperature or is cooked at a low heat.

Catherine Kerry says that her family never cooked chips in olive oil because the two didn't seem to go together. Ian Parmenter would never cook chips in extra virgin olive oil as he believes that the essence of cooking chips is to get the potatoes tasting right, not to have the oil tasting right. But if he is oven baking chips the Italian way, he uses a splash of olive oil and rosemary.

Rosa Matto believes that the oil should not dominate when it comes to cooking chips. She thinks that the potato loses its integrity when fried in olive oil. But she does use a good olive oil for potatoes *al forno*.

Ann Oliver, on the other hand, would always cook her chips in the finest extra virgin if she could afford it. She ate chips fried in olive oil in Cyprus and says they were fantastic. She had to cook her chips this way in Greece, as her landlady would bring her a bottle of olive oil every week. Ann was forced to use her oil frequently and in large amounts. Back in Australia, cooking chips in olive oil was regarded as unnecessary and extravagant. But as Ann puts it: 'Would you drink domestic champagne if you could afford Bollinger?'

Stefano Manfredi says that theory is no substitute for practice. He remembers VinItaly in Verona in 1988, where a group of Italy's highly regarded olive oil producers deep fried chips in extra virgin olive oil for the benefit of the Americans in attendance. The Americans declared that the chips were spectacular.

napoleon niarchos's recipes

Preserved olives

There are many different ways to preserve olives. Here are some popular methods, including Napoleon Niarchos's favourite recipes from a Greek village near Kalamata.

Green olives

Pick olives in the second month of autumn when they are yellow in colour. They should be very firm when squeezed. Place the olives in a container with plain water for at least 3 to 4 days. Change the water every 24 hours. Strain them and place on a clean plastic sheet to dry. Sprinkle them with salt, oregano, thyme and crushed orange skin. (Dry the orange skin in a moderate oven.) After 24 hours put the olives in a sterilised container and fill it with olive oil. The olives are ready to eat immediately. They may be a little bitter at first, but this is nothing to worry about as it is the natural aroma of the olives.

Green table olives

Pick olives when they are green and very firm, without any black spots. Crack them a bit with a small hammer. Place them in a container with fresh water. Change water every 24 hours. After 7 days drain the olives and place in preserving jars with a solution of boiled water with 10 per cent salt. The water should be red when the olives are drained. Mix in plenty of dill or wild fennel instead of herbs. Seal tightly. The olives will be ready to eat in 15 days.

Pink table olives

Pick olives when they are pink in colour. With a very sharp knife make three lengthwise incisions in each olive. Place in a container with fresh water for a week, changing the water every 24 hours. Drain the olives and place them in a container with a tight lid, preferably with a rubber seal. Boil enough water solution, with 10 per cent salt, to cover the olives. Boil for 15 minutes and allow to cool. Pour solution over the olives. Add a mixture of oregano, thyme, cumin and crushed dried orange skin to the container. Pour approximately 2 cups of olive oil on top of the olives. Seal and serve after 2 weeks.

Table olives

Pick olives when they are very firm and are mixed green and pink in colour.

Wash thoroughly and place in jars. Boil water with 10 per cent salt. Strain. Add the same herb mixture as used in the previous recipes. These olives will last for years.

Black olives

These olives are picked in the last month of autumn. Wash thoroughly and place in a container. Dissolve 200 grams of lime (oxide of calcium) in a separate bucket with 18 litres of water. Pour this mixture over olives and fill containers with clean water. Drain olives after 24 hours and wash the olives thoroughly (at least 3 or 4 times). Then place the olives in preserving containers. Mix with herbs. Boil water with 10 per cent salt and pour over olives, top with olive oil. These will be ready to eat in 2 weeks.

Using preserved olives either bought from the supermarket or pickled at home, olives can be 'dressed' with a number of different ingredients.

4 cloves garlic • 125 g soft white bread crumbs • 2 tbspn white wine vinegar • 4 to 5 tbspn olive oil • salt to taste • 1 to 2 tbspn water (if needed) • 50 g walnut or almonds, finely chopped (optional)

Skorthalia (Greek garlic sauce)

Peel and chop the garlic. Soak the bread crumbs for 10 minutes in a little water, then drain. Place the bread, garlic and vinegar in a blender and mix. Blend in oil in a trickle. Season with salt. If too thick add more water. The sauce should reach a mayonnaise-like consistency. Chopped almonds or walnuts can be added if desired. The flavour can be strengthened by adding more garlic. Serve with fried fish or vegetables or both.

300 g black olives • 100 g anchovy fillets • 100 g tuna in oil • 50 g capers • 1 clove garlic • 200 ml olive oil • cognac to taste

Tapenade

Stone the olives and pound them in a mortar or use a blender until they have been reduced to a paste. Pound or blend the drained anchovies, drained tuna, capers and garlic. Add Cognac to taste. Dribble in olive oil until you obtain a uniform paste. Serve as an appetiser on canapes made with wholemeal bread or toast.

Gazpacho

1 clove garlic, crushed • 75 g crustless day old bread • 1¹/₂ kg tomatoes, very red and ripe • 165 g cucumber • 155 g green capsicums • 8 tbspn vinegar • 8 tbspn olive oil • less than a tbspn of salt • 1 litre water
garnish: ¹/₂ cucumber per person, finely diced • ¹/₂ green capsicum per person, finely diced • 60 g stale bread, diced and fried • 2 large tomatoes, drained of water and seeds, diced

Slice the bread, capsicums and tomato. Add the water, vinegar, cucumber and garlic. Put aside and allow to mascerate for an hour. Put into a blender with olive oil and mix until it is a smooth puree. Put into a bowl, cover and chill. Serve in individual bowls with garnishes on the side. A bit of cumin may be added if desired.

Sopa de pao com tomate (Portuguese bread soup with tomato)

1 kg ripe tomatoes, seeded and chopped • 1 medium onion, chopped • 2 cloves garlic, crushed • 4 eggs • 400 g stale bread, cut into thin slices • 1 litre water • 6 tbspn olive oil

Heat the oil in a pan and gently fry the onion and garlic. Add the tomato and fry until it thickens (about 20 minutes). Add the water and salt and bring to the boil. Stir gently and drop the eggs in, letting them poach in the liquid. Put slices of bread in a soup bowl, place the eggs on top of the bread and add the rest of the soup. Serve very hot.

125 ml joseph olive oil • 3 cloves of garlic, chopped •
1/2 cup fresh basil leaves • 250 g stale continental bread,
sliced thinly • 2 litres chicken stock • 1 kg ripe tomatoes,
seeded and chopped

Pappa al pomodoro (bread and tomatoes)

In a saucepan sauté the garlic in the oil. Add bread slices and brown lightly on both sides. Add tomatoes and cook for a few minutes on high heat, stirring well with a wooden spoon. Then add chicken stock and basil and simmer, covered, over low heat for about 20 minutes. Taste for seasoning, turn off heat and rest for about an hour. Reheat and serve in bowls with plenty of olive oil drizzled over.

1 cup cracked green olives • 1 cup kalamata olives •
1/2 cup olive oil • 2 minced garlic cloves • 1/2 tspn cumin •
1/4 tspn paprika • 1/2 tspn harissa • 1 diced preserved lemon •
2 tbspn lemon juice • 1 tbspn chopped coriander •
1 tbspn fresh parsley.

Warm olives with preserved lemons

Place the olives in a saucepan and cover with water. Bring to a boil and immediately drain. Repeat process one more time. heat the olive oil in a small saucepan. Add the garlic, cumin, paprika, harissa (a spicy hot Moroccan condiment which may be purchased in a tube or small can from specialty food shops), preserved lemons, and olives. Cook over medium heat uncovered for one minute. Remove from the heat and place in a bowl. Add the lemon juice, coriander and parsley. Toss together.

Roasted capsicum salad

1 kg red capsicums • 6 tbspn olive oil • 1 kg tomatoes, washed peeled and drained of water and seeds • 2 cloves garlic • $^1/_2$ tspn ground cumin • salt and pepper

Halve the capsicums and grill until the skin is blackened. Peel them, remove seeds and cut into strips. Cut the tomatoes into small cubes and chop the garlic. Heat the oil in a frying-pan, add the garlic and let simmer without browning. Add the tomatoes and fry until their juice has evaporated. Add the strips of capsicum and simmer over a low heat for 30 minutes. Season with salt, pepper and cumin. Serve at room temperature.
Serves 6 to 8

don evangelista's
recipe

Fried black olives

handful of very ripe black olives straight from the tree • olive oil for frying • 2 whole red chillies • 6 whole garlic cloves

Fry for 2 to 3 minutes. Pour over extra oil at the finish.

joe grilli's
recipes

Panzanella – vineyard breakfast

Rub garlic onto slices of crusty bread. Sprinkle with diluted red wine vinegar. Drizzle with olive oil. Sprinkle with salt and freshly ground black pepper.

Pinzimonio (olive oil dip)

1 clove garlic • 180 ml olive oil • 60 ml red wine vinegar • sea salt and freshly ground black pepper to taste

Steep squashed garlic clove in oil for about one hour. Remove garlic. Add vinegar and salt and pepper to taste. Mix well to combine oil and vinegar. Serve as a dip with a selection of raw vegetables (celery, carrot, fennel, radish, mushrooms). This dip goes particularly well with globe artichokes boiled until slightly tender in lightly salted water. Individual leaves are dipped and only the tender flesh, heart and stem eaten.

Pancetta salad

8 to 10 thin slices of pancetta, cut into quarters • 1 large bowl of mixed salad leaves, washed and dried • $1/2$ orange capsicum, thinly sliced • 2 ripe tomatoes, cut into small pieces • 8 anchovy fillets, cut into small pieces • $3/4$ cup parmesan, shaved • olive oil as required • 4 to 5 tbspn red wine vinegar • pepper to taste

Fry pancetta in a small amount of oil until crispy. Place lettuce, capsicum, tomatoes, anchovies, and parmesan in a large bowl. Add cooked pancetta while still hot. Add about a third of a cup of olive oil. In the same pan that the pancetta was cooked in, warm up the vinegar. Add to the salad, along with freshly ground black pepper to taste. Toss salad well. Serve immediately with crusty bread.

Fennel and orange salad

oranges • fennel • black olives • extra virgin olive oil • red wine vinegar • salt and pepper to taste

Peel oranges and cut into round slices. Cut fennel into thin wedges. Place in a salad bowl with a handful of black olives. Dress with extra virgin olive oil and red wine vinegar. Season with salt and pepper.

Spaghetti aglio e olio (spaghetti with garlic and olive oil sauce)

500 g spaghetti • 3 cloves garlic, chopped • 2 red chillies, chopped (optional) • ¹/₂ cup joseph olive oil • salt and pepper to taste • chopped fresh parsley to garnish

Bring a pot of salted water to the boil and cook spaghetti until *al dente*. Drain. Meanwhile, gently fry the garlic and chilli in the oil in a heavy-based pan. As soon as the garlic starts to colour, add spaghetti and toss for a couple of minutes over heat. Season with salt and pepper to taste and serve sprinkled with parsley.

Bigoli in salsa

500 g bigoli (large spaghetti) • 4 large onions, thinly sliced • 20 anchovy fillets (small italian variety) • freshly ground black pepper to taste • olive oil as required

Cook pasta in plenty of salted boiling water until *al dente*. Drain well. Heat some olive oil in a large frypan, add onions and cook gently until soft. Add anchovy fillets and stir until they break up. Season with pepper to taste. Add some white wine if the mixture becomes too dry. Return pasta to pan and mix with the sauce. Add more olive oil if too dry. Serve with lots of grated parmigiano and continental bread.

Olive oil cake

5 egg yolks • 185 g sugar • 1 tbspn grated mixed orange and lemon peel • 125 ml joseph olive oil • 125 ml primo estate botrytis riesling • 125 g plain flour, sifted • ¹/₄ tspn salt • 7 egg whites • ¹/₂ tspn cream of tartar

Butter and flour a 20 cm cake pan and line with baking paper. Beat the egg yolks with half the sugar until pale and thick. Beat in the mixed peel, olive oil and riesling. Sift in the flour and salt and mix until just combined. Beat the egg whites with the cream of tartar until they hold stiff peaks then beat in the rest of the sugar. Fold the whites into the egg yolk mixture until well incorporated. Pour cake mixture into prepared pan and bake in a preheated 180°C oven for 20 minutes. Then lower the temperature to 150°C and cook for a further 20 minutes. Remove cake from the oven, cover with a round of buttered baking paper and let cool in the pan before turning out onto a wired rack. Dust cake with sifted icing sugar before serving.

russell jeavons's
recipes russell's kitchen
willunga

500 g almonds and/or hazelnuts • 100 g sesame seeds •
50 g coriander seeds • 50 g cumin seeds (or your favourite
aromatic seed) • salt and pepper to taste   **Dukkah**

Toast the nuts and seeds in a slow (100°C) oven until lightly coloured. Cool before milling the nuts coarsely, crushing the sesame seeds slightly, and crushing the coriander and cumin finely. A coffee grinder is ideal but a food processor should do. Mix it all up with a teaspoon of salt and quarter of a teaspoon of pepper. Add more to taste. To serve, dip good bread (see recipe below) into really good olive oil then into the dukkah.

To make really good bread 900 g unbleached bread flour • 300 g organic stone ground flour • 20 g salt • 25 g fresh compressed yeast • 700 ml rain or filtered water

Soak the yeast in 500 ml of water until it dissolves. Add to the flour and salt. Mix up a dough with the rest of the water, adjusting the temperature so the dough feels slightly warm. Coat the dough with oil and let it rise but not all the way. Knock it down, reform a ball, and let it rise again. A bit further this time, but not all the way. Gently form into two loaves and place them in an oiled tin (it is easiest this way), or on a well-floured tray. As they are rising strongly, place them in a 200°C oven. After ten minutes turn down to 180°C and cook for 40 to 60 minutes.

Water converting to steam rises the bread. Make sure the dough is as wet as possible while remaining manageable.

connie rotolo's
recipe
enoteca sileno
adelaide 1 kg eggplant (round) • ¹/₂ litre italian white wine vinegar • ¹/₂ litre water • sea salt • basil • 3 cloves garlic •

Melanzane sott'olio extra virgin olive oil • whole chillies (optional)
alla siciliana
(marinated
eggplant)

Peel the eggplant then slice thinly lengthways. Sprinkle with salt and place in layers in a stainless steel saucepan. Place a weighted plate on top for 12 hours. Squeeze out the brine. In a large pot bring the water and the vinegar to the boil, add the eggplant and boil for about 2 minutes. Drain and lie the eggplant on tea towels for 12 hours to dry. Pack into sterilised jars with garlic and basil, and whole chillies if desired. Cover with extra virgin olive oil and seal. These will keep in the refrigerator for up to 12 months. Always use clean utensils to remove the eggplant and top up the olive oil so it covers the eggplant. Use the eggplant as an antipasto. It is delicious with crusty Italian bread.

seb bosh's
recipes
sisco's on the pier
hobart

Calabaza alinada

1 kg butternut pumpkin, finely sliced • 1 tbspn parsley, finely chopped • 1 tbspn fresh thyme, finely chopped • 1 tbspn fresh rosemary, finely chopped • 1 tbspn garlic, finely chopped • 1 tbspn onion, finely chopped • 150 ml spanish sherry vinegar or balsamic vinegar • 200 ml olive oil

Fry the pumpkin slices in hot oil until golden brown. Drain oil and let cool. Add the finely chopped ingredients and the olive oil to the pumpkin and refrigerate overnight. Serve on a platter, drizzling all the liquid over the pumpkin. This is a great summertime dish to accompany meat or fish. If refrigerated, it will last for days and develop its flavour.

Escalivada

eggplant • red and green peppers • olive oil • salt and black pepper to taste

Choose the choicest eggplant and thick-skinned red and green peppers in equal amounts. Rub the vegetables, still with skin on, all over with olive oil as if you were giving them a massage. Place them on an open bar grill over hot embers. It is important not to flame the vegetables, and to continuously rotate them evenly until the skin becomes crisp and wants to peel off. When the vegetables become slightly softened remove them from the heat and peel them by hand. Cut the vegetables in half. Remove the caps from the peppers. Slice the vegetables lengthways about half a centimetre wide. Dress them on a serving platter and drizzle over liberal amounts of olive oil. Season with freshly ground black pepper and salt. These are great with roasted seasonal kid or rabbit.

Allioli

This sauce is used in Catalonia, Spain, to accompany almost every eating occasion. Traditionally a mortar and pestle are used to pound the garlic and emulsify the oil. It is said that you must be in a good mood to make allioli or it will curdle.
5 to 6 cloves of garlic, peeled • 2 egg yolks at room temperature • 600 ml olive oil • $1/2$ tspn salt • 1 tbspn parsley, chopped

In a mortar and pestle pound the garlic and salt until a paste is achieved. Add the egg yolks and stir at a constant speed, always in the one direction. When egg yolks have emulsified the garlic, start drizzling oil very slowly. Stop the drizzling every now and then to allow the egg to catch up with the emulsification. Never stop stirring. Keep on drizzling until you have achieved a thick mixture. Stir in the parsley before serving. You can make lots of variations depending on what you intend to serve the allioli with. Lemon juice, finely chopped apple or honey can be added for different flavours.

harvesting the grove

'When I started out I didn't know much about olives and making oil. I asked Lew Kathreptis what he knew about pressing oil, and he said that as a kid he had heard that you should take the olive "on the flame", that is, when they are half-green, half-black. That's how I took them and that's how I like them. If I wanted to do something different I would have to experiment with flavours.' **Jane Ferrari**

It is a commonplace to mention the enormous changes wrought in Australian society by post-war European migration. Cappucino, exotic meats, spicy dishes, garlic, Italian, Greek, Turkish, French, Vietnamese and other national restaurants … all these and much more arrived with the migrants to transform the dull steak and cake, pies and beer landscape of Australian social life and cuisine. So revolutionary was the general change, that it is easy to overlook some of its many smaller details – the pieces that make up the larger and colourful mosaic. One of these components – as familiar now as it was unheard of some years ago – is olive oil. Australia of the 1990s and the new millennium is olive oil conscious and this means not only changes in the kitchen, in restaurants, delicatessens, markets and personal tastes, but also possible economic opportunity and agricultural change of a kind as stunning as the Australian wine industry has brought about on the landscape, in our cities and in the country's export profile. It is time now to consider olive oil as a production.

Australia imports about $87,000,000 worth of olive oil each year and this figure is increasing. So a large potential local market exists already, as does a smaller boutique market where some local oils are fetching quite high prices.

It is estimated that about 350,000 olive trees were sold in Australia in 1995-96, with 200,000 being planted just in New South Wales. Whether this intensive planting is something of a frenzy, driven by promise of profit in a new field, or whether Australia as an olive oil market fully justifies such radical expansion are questions to which there are as yet no clear answers. Or rather, the answers are different depending on who is asked.

In general, however, there do seem to be reasons for cautious optimism about an Australian olive oil industry. The health-conscious Japanese are showing an interest in olive oil, and Italy, the world's largest olive oil consumer, is a net importer. So there is also a potential export market. Moreover, premium oils recently exported have been well received. With the imminent reduction in European Union subsidies to olive farmers, Australian oils will become more competitive.

This incipient momentum is being intensified by Australia's rapidly developing 'green and clean image' – a spin-off from the excellent reputation of the Australian wine industry, which has conquered the world by combining modern science and technology with old world tradition.

All this augurs well for a successful Australian olive oil industry. There are, as always, some difficulties. The oil market is not homogeneous. The bulk supermarkets can compete directly with cheap seed oils which can be manipulated to match olive oil superficially in a number of its features. This market is driven primarily by costs and margins that only multinationals and corporate agribusiness enterprises can sustain. And the tourist market, with quaint bottles of olive oil topped by rustic cloth and a bow of silk, has only so much space and cannot support more than a local cottage industry.

Nevertheless, Australian olive oil producers can be encouraged by the upmarket swing to high-quality varietal oil on the part of Italian consumers, who account for more than half of all the sales. They are discerning consumers who are motivated by more than price alone. This market can be cultivated in Australia and overseas by the middle section of the Australian olive oil industry, which can produce high-quality, varietal, estate-bottled oils, perhaps, in time, with a distinctive regional ethos. This market suits the style of many of the people who have already been drawn to olive growing and oil production in Australia and is one of several causes for optimism about the industry's future.

producers

jane ferrari

ferrari

Jane's Ferrari Cold Pressed Extra Virgin Olive Oil is acclaimed by some of Australia's top chefs. Surprisingly, she only started making olive oil four years ago. As a wine maker, Jane has always kept company with chefs. Her father is Italian and she has always had olive oil in the house. She remembers visiting her grandmother's house in Italy, where glass containers of olive oil were kept wrapped in wicker under the house. Jane's father was particularly fond of fresh fennel dipped in olive oil and salt.

Ten years ago Jane met Lew Kathreptis and started hanging out in the kitchen at Mezes restaurant in Adelaide. Jane says that it was Lew who sparked her interest in the food world.

A few years later, Jane's boss at Yalumba sent her a memo asking her to do some research into olive trees and olive oil. There were a hundred or so olive trees growing wild on the Yalumba property. Many of these had been brought back from abroad thirty or forty years ago. Some of them were proper varietals from Italy or Spain, but others were unidentifiable.

Jane's research did not amount to much. Then she went to work at Rockford's winery, remaining good friends with the people at Yalumba. With their agreement, Jane took a chainsaw to the trees on the Yalumba property. In their wild form the trees had been producing a lot of fruit, but the olives were small, without much flesh. After Jane started pruning the trees, they produced a more even distribution of bigger fruit that started to take on the varietal characteristics of the tree. 'When I started out I didn't know much about olives and making oil. I asked Lew Kathreptis what he knew about pressing oil, and he said that as a kid he had heard that you should take the olive "on the flame", that is, when they are half-green, half-black. That's how I took them and that's how I like them. If I wanted to do something different I would have to experiment with flavours.'

The parallels between the grape vine and the olive tree helped Jane immensely. She simply applied the practice of the viticulture world to olives: 'I expect olives are a lot like grapes, they accumulate oil at a certain rate and they accumulate flavour at a certain rate and the two are not necessarily co-related. If you leave them late you'll get more oil, but the flavour won't be there. If you pick them early you'll get bugger all oil, and the flavour will be horrible anyway.'

The first year that Jane picked olives, she only ended up with half a sugar bag of them, which seemed a lot to her. She went to Joe Bagnato's press house where the proprietors laughed their heads off. Jane wasn't to know that this was a very small quantity of olives for extracting oil, but she did know Italians, and she had taken along a few bottles of wine. After the owners had finished laughing and finished the wine, they told Jane that they would leave the mats in place after the day's pressing so she could do her olives. She made two flagons of oil.

Jane presented her oil to Lew, who thought it was quite good, though he didn't quite believe that she had made it. This encouraged Jane, who discovered more olive trees in the Barossa Valley and, thinking grapes again – the same climate, the same soil on that side of the valley – she combined the fruit with the pickings from Yalumba. She sent some of the resultant oil to Simon Johnson, purveyor of fine foods, who was impressed, and to Stefano Manfredi, who said it 'wasn't bad'. And, as Jane says, 'coming from Stefano that's pretty good!'

The next year Jane produced between 300 and 400 bottles of oil. In

'At the press house you
have to wait for three or
four hours. You get to talk
to everyone who has come
in with their olives, all
picked at different stages
of ripeness. They all come
out as different types of
oil and you can taste them.
At the Bagnato's press they
have a wood-fired oven, they
bake their own bread, they
kill their own pig once a
year and make salami - it's
part of a bigger world.
You've got to be involved
and be part of the process.
You can't do that sitting
in a sterile laboratory,
analysing what flavour peaks
or what tannins you've got
in your oil.'

1995, Stephanie Alexander announced at a master class that Ferrari oil was wonderful. Jane says that Stephanie's comments really gave her a boost to keep going.

Jane picks her olives by hand and treats them gently. As she puts it, you wouldn't bounce an orange on the ground several times before you eat it, so why do that with olives. She takes the olives to the press as quickly as possible so that the olives are in the best possible condition.

Jane has stuck with traditional pressing, because she feels she can control each batch. She can see exactly what is happening, and she knows what temperature is being used because she can feel it. It is easy for her to see the condition of the paste on the mats, and the oil coming off.

The press house has taught Jane everything she knows about making olive oil. She thinks it is important not to get too technical, and has never been to a lecture on olive oil production.

Jane believes that the intuitive, hands-on approach produces oils with a better flavour than those that are produced under perfect technical conditions. She considers her oil as an ingredient, not just something to cook in. She says that it is an adjunct, a flavour in itself, and recommends using it with green vegetables or as the base for an interesting mustard sauce.

Jane is now back at Yalumba, and her boss says that in ten years' time any winery that has a heart will also have an olive grove. Yalumba are planting varietals at a rate of knots. Grapes are picked in the summer, and olives are picked in the winter, so the two fruits complement each other.

The demand for Jane's oil is now so great that several retailers have phoned her to say they will take all the oil she can produce. Each year it will be available at Yalumba cellar door when it is released in October.

emmanuel giakoumis and mark lloyd

coriole

Emmanuel Giakoumis came to Australia from Greece in 1955. When he arrived in Adelaide, he worked as an electrician and a motor mechanic. In 1956 he began to pick olives around Adelaide and sold them to the Star Grocery for preserving.

In 1962, Emmanuel bought his own processing machine. He used the old method of oil extraction and had trouble selling the olive oil. The processing method was very primitive – it was the method practised in Greece when he left. The oil was hot and took a long time to process, making it quite heavy. The Greek community in Adelaide had become used to vegetable oil, and had lost the taste for heavy, acidic olive oil.

Emmanuel travelled to America, Spain and Greece in 1972, where he explored new ideas and new machinery. In 1975, he bought a new processing plant, and after that he had no trouble selling the oil. He bought some land in McLaren Vale and started his own business producing oil and pickled olives. His property had twenty varieties of olives and he would mix them with olives from people in Willunga and Port Pirie.

Mark Lloyd became interested in olive oil in 1979 when he travelled through Greece in December and January. The places that interested him the most were the oil factories which are normally closed during the tourist season. Mark even worked in an olive oil factory in Crete. Back in McLaren Vale he was told that there was a local press run by Emmanuel Giakoumis. 'I couldn't believe it, it was the exactly the same as those in Greece. The same hospitality. It was a separate little culture.'

That was how the Lloyd family met Emmanuel, and how Guy Lloyd from Coriole came to buy Emmanuel's land, which had once belonged to the Hardy family. The Hardy's had planted olive trees as boundaries to their vineyards 120 years ago. About sixty years ago, they had replaced the vines with olives.

Emmanuel stayed on as manager for the Lloyds until a few years ago.

The photograph on the opposite page shows the harvesting of Kalamata olives at McLaren Vale Olive Groves. This company produces 1500 litres of family reserve olive oil a year under its own label.

McLaren Vale is full of olive trees, many self-seeded from the established groves in the area. Emmanuel co-ordinates the picking of the olives, combining wild olives from around the property and from their young olive grove. The olives are then taken to one of the continual presses in Adelaide. In his view, if olive farmers want to be profitable, they should not pick by hand.

Emmanuel realises that each variety of olive produces different oil and requires different processing. He says that some olives are processed well with the mat method, but that it is not suitable for others because it is hard to get the oil out. Some people used to leave the olives for two or three weeks before processing, but Emmanuel says that this is not a good idea because in that time the acidity of the oil will increase. He advises people to 'harvest today and process tomorrow'.

Olives ripen at different stages, so picking is difficult. Emmanuel likes to pick when the olives are blackish. He processes these olives straight away, processes the other olives when they are ready, and then blends the oil. He thinks Verdale is the best olive and that the oil from Verdale with a 50 per cent mix of Mission produces a sublime oil.

Emmanuel has been in the olive business for many years and claims he learnt a lot by trial and error. He now works as a consultant, advising on the planting of new olive groves in South Australia. He also produces oil for Coriole and preserves Kalamata olives, which he sells under the Southern Valley Oil Products label. Mark Lloyd says of his transition: 'At sixty-eight years of age Emmanuel became a chemist. He's fantastic, he is there

with burettes, solutions, and all the gear. It means that he can check quality, make comparisons.'

In 1996, Coriole produced 3500 litres of olive oil. They are not interested in huge production. They are more concerned with understanding the product and getting the quality as high as possible. Mark feels that each year he is getting a better product: 'You are limited by what varieties you have. We have only seriously been producing Coriole for the last couple of years. It's a matter of getting the fruit in at the right time. From 1997, we will start to produce an extra special oil as well as our extra virgin. Times have changed. In 1989, people would come into the cellar and be incredulous of olive oil. They would say, "What is this doing here? Isn't this what the Vet told me to use in my dog's ears?" Their attitude has completely changed in four years.'

Coriole also played a part in starting the craze for dukkah. A few years ago they organised a lunch at the Salopian Inn for the International Olive Oil Council. Brigita Turniski contributed dukkah, which she took from a Claudia Roden recipe which in turn was modified from an Egyptian recipe. Russell Jeavons later developed his own version to reflect the character of McLaren Vale by using local produce. He claims to have converted even the sceptics. Emmanuel Giakoumis and Vince Scarfo, who produce Diana Olive Oil, are devotees.

'We always put the year of vintage on the Coriole Extra Virgin Oil label. We are chasing a real freshness, a real characteristic oil. It's got a character that is related to the material you take it from, akin to wines. What we are after is something that is fresh and expressive of the fruit available, something that has not been adversely affected by picking or processing.'

joe grilli

joseph

Joe grew up as a first generation Australian in Adelaide. Both his parents were born in Italy, and Joe took olive oil for granted while he was growing up. During the 1980s he took his first trip to Italy, where he saw the Tuscan vineyards producing an olive oil with the same label as their wine.

Joe says that having the vintage on labels for olive oil is just common sense. A consumer should look for something to indicate the harvest, such as a use-by date.

Joe's first olive oil season was in 1989. Joseph Olive Oil does not come from a particular grove. Joe tapped into the network of Greek and Italian people he grew up with. The first olive grower Joe approached was the family supplier, Jim the Greek. Joe didn't even know Jim's surname. In Joe's district there are thousands of olive trees on various properties, many of which were planted as windbreaks.

The olives Joe uses are different varieties of different ages, but they all come from the same area on the Adelaide Plains – Virginia, Two Wells, Gawler River and the Adelaide metropolitan area. Overall, Joe estimates that anything from 1500 to 3000 tonnes of olives come in each season. The most prominent variety is Verdale.

Joe takes his olives to four different presses in Adelaide. His Foothills Extra Virgin Olive Oil comes from a small parcel of olives from Alden and Beaumont, remnants of the old Davenport groves: 'We pressed those olives and the oil was of a different style – different colour oil, different flavour. I decided to keep that batch separate.'

Joe has produced four vintages of the Foothills oil. It has a green lustre, a peppery taste with just a slight bitterness, and a cleansing finish. Joe says

'By putting a vintage on labels you are telling people how fresh the oil is, and you are allowing people to start noticing the differences between vintages. Australians have labelled their wines with freshness and honesty, without ambiguity. Olive oil can follow that concept.'

that the green banana character of the oil could be a regional characteristic.

Any olives that aren't used in the Foothills oil go into Joe's other oils. He uses the traditional presses for these olives. It is a long process with lots of tiny batches.

Joe's olives are picked by hand, the long, hard old-fashioned way. His Foothill olives are hand-picked by a retired Calabrian man, who has been picking olives for more than twenty years. Joe declares that in the modern olive oil industry technology is not the whole answer. He says that people may be disappointed if they grasp technology as their saviour. He learnt his lesson with wine. On the other hand, he notes, the technology of mechanical harvesting will improve the quality of an oil because the producer will be able to harvest enough to go to press the same day.

Joe's extra virgin oil is ripe and fruity, with a strong olive fruit character: 'It's a distillation of the climate, the random varieties and of the people and the way they handle the olives. All of that is in a bottle of Joseph Extra Virgin Olive Oil. The term *terroir* can be used much more correctly for oil than wine because the oil is an expression of all those factors. Compared with wine there is almost no technology involved. Once the oil is cold pressed, it sits in a stainless steel tank and is bottled from that tank. There is no racking, refining, filtering, corrections or addition of preservatives. There are analogies with the wine industry, though. Like the old vine shiraz and grenach vines, people are belatedly starting to realise how valuable the old olive trees are.'

Joe does not like to talk a lot about the oil processing because he thinks it is simple: 'I live by my wits. As each batch comes out of the press I use my nose and my palate. If a batch doesn't have fresh olive character, it isn't used and the grower gets to keep that oil. In Australia there is really

'I try to bring out the strong, fresh fruit character of the olives, and use the continuous modern press for these because I want that pristine fruit flavour.'

only cold pressed oil. People get too technical. Thirty-five degrees compared to twenty-nine degrees – big deal!'

Annually Joe crushes sixty tonnes of olives in total – twenty tonnes for the Foothills and forty tonnes from everywhere else. He bottled 6000 litres in 1996, a year when the olive trees really cropped. By the end of April there were no bottles left, and that was with hardly any marketing.

Joe has recently planted 500 new trees and is exploring modern growing ideas. His philosophy is that there is no such thing as a bad olive. He believes that any fresh olive picked at the right time will make a good oil, and that different varieties just make for different characters. He thinks that new varieties will enable growers to produce a higher yield per hectare, costs will be cut, and processing equipment will improve.

Joe's vision is for every good Australian kitchen to have a selection of oils so that people can select the sort of oils they will use with different foods. Joe uses the greener Foothills oil, with its highly toned olive character, for example, in salads and with any green steamed vegetables. He recommends the riper, fruitier, softer Joseph Extra Virgin for pasta dishes: 'A green oil doesn't gel as much as a softer, fruitier oil. I love the white flesh of a char-grilled fish with a soft fruity oil poured over it. It just works. Use oil in cooking and then add a little bit of fresh oil at the end while the food is cooling down. This ties up the flavours. The oil conveys the flavours of the other ingredients to our senses.'

don evangelista

greenfields

Olives have always been a part of Don Evangelista's life. He first came to Australia alone from Calabria in southern Italy in 1954, working in a factory for seven years until he started working as a builder.

When Don arrived in Adelaide he had no expectations about the state of the olive oil industry there but was pleased to find olive trees growing around the city. He made no trips to the shops for olive oil. Instead he picked olives from the Adelaide Hills each year and took them to Samuel Danvenport's old press at Beaumont. But he also found out about the other presses around Adelaide. He discovered one on Morialta Road, one at Flinders Park, and one at Port Adelaide. These were all run by Greeks. In the 1960s a good modern press was set up at Brompton by Italians.

Around this time Kevin Powell and the Trim brothers bought out what used to be called the Adelaide Olive Oil Company at Magill and, in 1974, Don bought a ten acre parcel of land from them. His property was situated on Kensington Road in Wattle Park. He still tends the olives on this land.

In 1991, recognising the need for good olive oil in Australia, Don established the Greenfields Olive Oil Company with the first automatic plant. He is happy to cater for everyone, but it is mainly South Australians and Victorians who use the plant. He does not sell oil himself, just makes enough for his own needs.

At Don's plant, everybody's batch is processed separately. The machine can work on any quantity. There is no minimum quantity, but there is a minimum fee. It costs the same to process 10 kilograms as it does to process 300 kilograms of olives.

Don believes that cold pressed olive oil does not exist: 'You must use some heat to produce oil. Different varieties of olives will produce different flavoured oil, but the difference will not be great. The biggest difference comes from the time of picking the olives and how long they are left before pressing. Oil pressed early in the season, when olives are green, is very

'It is the flavour and goodness that makes olive oil special. It is as good as any lotion you can use on your skin or your hair. Olive oil brings bread to life and gives you goodness to keep you going. If you just have bread and olive oil you will survive quite well.'

strong and sometimes bitter. The younger the olive, the better the fruit; the older the olive, the more oil it produces.

geoff and lynette winfield

toscana

Geoff's grandfather was granted land in the Grampian district of Victoria in 1872 by the Henty brothers. A public company, the Grampians Olive Plantation, bought the land in 1943 for olive groves. Geoff's first job when he left school in 1956 was working at the grove.

In 1976, Geoff and Lynette bought a native flower farm. Soon after they bought it, the land was compulsorily acquired by National Parks. When the Toscana plantation came up for sale, the couple decided to buy it. They intended to bulldoze it so they could grow flowers. But in 1988 Stephanie Alexander visited them and wrote an article about their olive grove for the *Age* newspaper in Melbourne. They decided not to pull the trees out. They realise now that if they had done so it would have been a tragedy.

The Winfields were not happy with the quality of oil they produced when they first started and decided to go to Italy in 1989 to study the cultivation of olives and the production of olive oil; they came back with a new press.

Today, although the Winfields have 1300 acres with 38,000 trees and twenty-seven varieties, they can not keep up with demand for their olive oil. They produce between 30,000 and 50,000 litres of it a year, which they sell direct to the public by mail order. Toscana is said to be the largest olive plantation in the southern hemisphere.

Geoff Winfield says that, although they have a mechanical shaker buried somewhere in mothballs, they harvest the olives by taking their

The Winfields have the largest olive press in Victoria. People take their olives to Toscana for pressing from as far away as Young in New South Wales.

frustrations out on the olive trees. The land is too wet in winter to use mechanical means.

Geoff and Lynette Winfield have been invited to export their oil to California, Italy and Germany. But they have rejected the idea because it would mean that they would have to double their output.

luigi bazzani

olea

Luigi Bazzarni came to Australia in 1952 and has been growing olives in Western Australia since 1954. As a young man he studied at agricultural college and worked in a nursery. His family has grown olives in Tuscany for 700 years.

In 1956, Luigi founded the Olea Nursery in Perth and has recently moved to the Margaret River district. He has bred his own olives and he is known as one of the best suppliers in Australia.

michael burr

beetaloo
olive grove

On an impulse in 1976, Michael planted his first olive trees in the harsh bushland setting of the southern Flinders Ranges with the vague notion that they would provide a retirement activity and income, as well as an enjoyable way of life. Fifteen years later it became obvious to him that things had to change if his grove was to become economical.

Michael began to study the olive by reading and observing at first-hand the practices in Spain, Italy, Greece, France, Portugal and Turkey. He also visited the many old groves in Australia and rediscovered its colonial olive history.

Michael's concern for the many newcomers who seem destined to follow his path induced him to publish his observations in a rough manual

'I regret the dilution of the old ways, but I am excited by the prospect of Australian technology establishing its olive oil industry as a world leader.'
Joe Grilli

'Olives ripen at different stages, so picking is difficult. I like to pick when the olives are blackish. I process these olives straight away, the others when they are ready, and then blend the oil.'
Emmannuel Giokoumis

entitled *Australian Olives, a guide for growers and producers of virgin oils*, not to discourage them but rather to point out some pitfalls and the necessary steps to success. In it Michael Burr recommends combining the best of tradition with the available modern technology, in much the same way as the Australian wine industry has done – with luck with a similar outcome to the way in which the new world excels the old. It is his belief that a book like *Extra Virgin* should help the user of olive oils to better appreciate the complexities of this unique, mysterious, divine and, of necessity, expensive fruit juice.

the cycle

Despite its seemingly uneventful life, the ever dull-green olive tree goes through an active yearly life cycle.

winter

Olive trees may be harvested late in to winter, either because the trees are late ripeners or because the farmers are late with their picking. They are usually then pruned. Olives prefer fertile, well-aerated and well-drained soil. During the winter months, the next year's buds start forming on the trees. If a tree suffers a hot dry winter instead of a cold wet one, it may bear little fruit the following season.

spring

The buds that are destined to become fruit – the others become woody growths or nothing – develop into tiny cream-coloured flowers. These flowers are receptive to the male pollen from another olive tree or, in some varieties, from their own flowers. Even the species that are self-fertile bear better crops following cross-pollination. The pollen is carried on the wind rather than by insects, which explains why the flowers are not big and brightly coloured. The flowers can remain fertile for anywhere between several hours and several days. Pollination can be interfered with by adverse spring weather, such as wind, hail, rain, or heat with water stress.

Although some of the olive fruit will fall off before ripening, the rest will go on to maturity. This process is aided by adequate nutrition and moisture, so the farmer needs to pay special attention to fertilisers and irrigation during these months.

summer

The stone forms in the fruit and begins to harden. The flesh and oil accumulate rapidly. As the quantity of oil continues to increase in the fruit, some of the desirable antioxidising and chemicals responsible for flavours diminish. The acidity rises with ripening, and consequently farmers will pick their olives early if they are concerned with quality rather than quantity.

A black scale – similar to citrus scale – occurs everywhere on olive trees. The scale reproduces during summer and, if this reproduction is not controlled, will drain the tree's vitality and predispose it to a sooty black fungus. Scale can usually be contained by spraying the tree with a white mineral oil that is acceptable in organic farming circles.

autumn

The fruit begins to be ready for harvesting. This was once an important family ritual, with the extended family gathering to pick, press and maybe prune the trees. Nowadays, the commercial farmer needs machinery to remain economically viable. In traditional groves, the yearly round of tasks demanded about four hundred hours per hectare, of which 70 per cent was for manual harvesting. In a modern grove with full mechanisation, this has been reduced to forty hours. So if it is the romance of an olive grove you are seeking, keep it small!

Because of its association with Biblical lands, people incorrectly assume that the olive favours a dry, desert climate. Although olive trees can survive in harsh conditions, they are unlikely to bear fruit of quality in commercial quantities.

For commercial fruit production the olive needs a mild, Mediterranean climate with cold wet winters and warm summers. Mild weather is important as frosts and strong winds are detrimental to important stages of the growth cycle. Surprisingly, heat of 30° C for more than three days brings oil production in the fruit to a halt. To form fruit, the tree needs to experience chilling of maybe 1500 hours at below 5°C during winter.

cultivating the olive

The Ancients believed that olives needed to be close to the sea to grow successfully. This is not so, but the belief may have been a reflection of the modulating effect of a body of water on temperature. In Australia, olives are being grown in all states and territories. It will be interesting to follow the progress of those in Central Australia as well as those in the sub-tropics and mountains to see the differences in yield.

Usually viral and fungal diseases become more prevalent in humid zones, especially when groves are dense. There are already unconfirmed reports of an olive fly with maggots, similar to the fruit fly, being detected in olive groves in the eastern states of Australia.

As a general rule, soil that is good for grapes is good for olives.

Although there are countless numbers of olives clinging to rocky barren hillsides – it was common practice to put olives on non-arable 'goat' country in Mediterranean countries – olives prefer fertile soil, just like most other fruit trees.

Olive trees dislike having 'wet feet' in poorly drained soil in which they fail to thrive and are prone to disease. Clay soils can also be a problem because they withhold moisture and nutrition from the tree. Such soil will also shrink and expand, causing damage to the roots of the tree. Some Australian soils are shallow and infertile, and they may be excessively acidic, which can make it difficult for the plant to survive.

The terraces of olives on the Greek islands are picturesque, but they are not negotiable by a mechanical harvester. For a modern commercial grove, the land needs to be relatively flat with enough room for ready access by farm machinery.

Although it can survive considerable water deprivation, it needs adequate moisture at the key stages of fruit formation in order to produce reliable commercial quantities of fruit. As natural rainfall is unpredictable, the serious olive grower must be ready to provide supplementary water by irrigation from time to time, especially during the tree's first five years.

Irrigation alters the content and composition of the oil from the olive as well as the weight of the fruit. A farmer who is selling table olives by weight will want to sell heavy fruit. For olives that are grown for their oil, farmers should understand the responses to irrigation of the varieties of olive tree they are growing.

Many areas of Australia have a salinity problem, or risk developing one if irrigation is practised regularly. Fortunately, the olive is able to thrive

Coriole played a part in starting the craze for dukkah. A few years ago they organised a lunch at the Salopian Inn for the International Olive Oil Council. Brigita Turnisky contributed dukkah, which she took from one of Claudia Roden's recipes.

'There are analogies with the wine industry. Like the old vine shiraz and grenach vines, people are belatedly starting to realise how valuable the old olive trees are.'
Joe Grilli

and bear fruit in the face of considerable salinity if the ground is well pre-pared and managed. In Israel, it has been shown that for some varieties the tree grown under extremely salty conditions is smaller than one grown under non-salty conditions, but the quantity and quality of oil produced is improved.

Regional water resource management with constraints on use is becoming an important feature of primary production in Australia, and people aspiring to become commercial olive growers need to take this into account. Those already growing may need to become more sophisticated in monitoring their water use – it is likely that, as with grape vines, many people over-water olive trees.

The yearly production of new wood and fruit on an olive tree requires water, air, sunlight and nutrients from the soil. Eventually the soil becomes depleted by constant 'mining', so if any form of agriculture is to be sustained, a land management strategy to replenish, or increase, the level of soil nutrients is required.

A proportion of new growers are adopting organic farming methods for their olives with the health-conscious consumer in mind. Market research shows that health considerations are already significant for buyers of higher quality oils. At the moment Australia believes it has a 'green and clean' image, and this is seen as a competitive edge when broaching the export market.

The organic practices of covering crops with green manure, mulching rather than tilling, and avoiding powerful synthetic weedicides and pesticides are the most likely to maintain the soil's fertility in the long run. But fertiliser from an external source will be essential if the object is to be commercial. Recent reports from Spain show a 68 per

'My philosophy is that there is no such thing as a bad olive. Any fresh olive picked at the right time will make a good oil.'
Joe Grilli

cent increase in the olive crop from the addition of composted urban waste.

From time to time, there will be insect predators that need to be eradicated. Although black scale (similar to citrus scale) is endemic to olives and needs to be controlled by yearly spraying with simple and acceptable white oil, other predators will be more resistant. In the eastern states, the Olive Lace Bug is creating havoc. Organic farmers have to deal with these bugs using organic methods, which are expensive and explain why organic olives are more expensive than non-organic ones.

Testing of Australian oils for chemical contamination has revealed only tiny amounts of halogens, and these are thought to have come from chlorinated water used in the extraction process.

The long-life olive is reasonably slow to mature. Tradition holds that it takes five years or more before these varieties bear even a reasonable crop, and much 'patient capital' is needed to develop a grove. Sir Samuel Davenport urged his fellow South Australian colonists to plant olives with the expectation of crops in three years, and recent experience with vigorous nursery plants and encouragement of growth using copious amounts of water and fertiliser suggest that he was right.

Unfortunately, however, it appears likely that the use of fertilisers to promote growth is one of the triggers that sets the olive tree into a sequence of alternate year bearing – heavy crops one year and little the next – which is inefficient from many points of view. The initial excessive growth of wood hampers the development of fruit in that year, but the tree over-responds, producing an excessive fruit crop in the following season and then little the next, and so on, out of kilter. Some varieties are more prone to alternate year bearing than others, and the various techniques to modulate the fluctuations – mainly by pruning excess growth or chemically reducing the excessive fruit load – have had only limited success.

When talking about yields it is important to use cumulative figures to allow for such fluctuations and from seasonal variations. In Australia, a conventional, irrigated olive tree will produce on average over the years of about 50 kilograms of olives each year, statistically speaking.

Before modern irrigation and fertilisers were widely available, the relatively shallow (70 centimetre) rooted olive trees were planted nine to ten metres apart to avoid competition for water and nutrients. Each tree often had a cluster of three, four or more trunks – the olive is really a big bush anyway, and keeps trying to revert. These forest giants were a challenge to pick and were inefficient, because much of the tissue was supportive rather than fruit-bearing wood.

With a move to more intensive cultivation, the trees were grown closer together and the picking made easier by controlling the size and shape of the tree through pruning and training. Traditionally the shape was that of a hollow vase or cocktail glass. This allowed easy access to the fruit and also light and air penetration.

As land prices and labour costs have increased, cultivation has become more intense. A system called 'monoconical intensive farming' was developed with the aim of moving towards maximum mechanical harvesting and pruning. Under this system the trees are grown with just one straight trunk that is clear to about one metre and topped by foliage in the shape of a Christmas tree.

These monoconical trees are grown close together – down to three metres between trees in rows six metres apart. Under this system of planting, it is possible to prune the outsides of the trees that face the row with a machine like a big suspended lawn mower.

With smaller trees of either shape it is then possible to grow from 250 to 350 trees on each hectare. The single trunk allows the use of a tree shaker for harvesting. These smaller, closely planted trees are then irrigated and fertilised, just like any other plant crop.

In 1988 Stephanie Alexander visited Toscana and wrote an article about their olive grove for the *Age* newspaper in Melbourne. They realise now that it would have been a tragedy to pull out the trees.

Recently there have been attempts to push this intensification to the limits by growing dwarf trees as a hedgerow. As with grapes the idea is then to harvest mechanically with an overhead machine that straddles the row. There seems to be some difficulty in putting this idea into practice with olives.

How and when should the fruit crop be harvested? Some people carry nostalgic memories of the bucolic frolic as happy extended families joined together to gather in the season's olives for their yearly supply of oil. While hobby olive farmers may still enjoy such harvests, the modern commercial reality is different.

Manual harvesting accounted for up to 70 per cent of the hours needed to operate a traditional grove, and this is prohibitive for commercial farmers who are paying hired labour. This has led farmers to grow trees in ways that are suitable for mechanical harvesting.

'The younger the olive, the better the fruit; the older the olive, the more oil it produces.'

Don Evangelista

There have been many attempts to improve the efficiency of manual picking since the North African women wore goat's horns on their fingers in ancient times. But generally the hand-held gadgets are more trouble than they are worth. The traditional beating of the tree damages the wood's tissue and probably the next year's crop, not to mention the fruit. It is as outdated as the saying, 'Your wife, your dog and the olive tree, the more you beat them, the better they be.'

These days the tree is grown with a single straight trunk up to about one metre so that the hydraulic pincers of the mechanical shaker can clamp on to it. This is unnatural as the olive is really a bush and wants to grow with a maze of multiple trunks. It has been said of modern olive cultivation that it is time to pull and replant when the tree shakes the tractor rather than the other way round.

Future harvesting will no doubt be done mostly on a contract basis by huge impressive machines that can shake 80 per cent of the olives off suitably grown trees – in straight lines on flat land – at the staggering rate of three trees each minute. At a demonstration of one of these machines in Adelaide, the overheard question was, 'Did the ground shake for you too?'

Picking the best time to harvest olives – as with grapes – requires experience, skill and intuition. The oil content increases the longer the fruit is allowed to hang on, but the acidity also increases, while the natural antioxidants and taste compounds diminish. There is also a progressive loss from windfalls and bird predation, leading to the adage, 'He who wants all the olives, does not get all the oil.'

These factors have led to differing regional practices and different styles of oil. In Calabria, in the south of Italy, the fruit is allowed to ripen until it falls on the ground and the oil is sweet and smooth. In the north, in Tuscany, the fruit is picked while it is half-green and the oil is feisty, even fiery, fruity, bitter and pungent. The early picked oil is rich in antioxidants, pigments and flavour compounds, which give it the sought-after 'frutato'.

In Tuscany it was said that, after pruning, 'you should be able to throw your cap through the tree'. In Spain it was said that 'a bird should be able to fly through the tree'. In Greece it was that 'the tree has to be able to breathe'.

Although the assertive Tuscan oil will keep better, it is something of an acquired taste, and most newcomers prefer the bland styles even though they do not keep as well because they are already on the way to inevitable oxidation and rancidity. History tells us that the early picking in the north

probably started as a way of avoiding crop losses from early cold weather, rather than as a preference for the bold robust green oil that is now in fashion.

As commercial laboratory services develop to allow olive oil producers to have the quality of their oil tested, it is also likely that tests of oil composition and content during ripening will help with the decision of when to harvest.

Early European settlers brought many selected varieties of olive to Australia. Many of these went feral, and through sexual crossbreeding have produced some well-adapted offspring.

Trying to select appropriate varieties is often difficult for olive growers. Many of the varieties that they desire are not available, and most of the names of varieties have been confused or replaced, so that there are many synonyms of any one variety. To this have been added more recent imports, some of them illegal, with their synonyms. Only those varieties that have been introduced strictly under quarantine regulations are able to be identified with certainty.

Even the best botanists make errors in identifying olive trees by their external features. Fortunately, Australian scientists are at the cutting edge in developing DNA fingerprinting techniques, and at the moment they can tell when two similar looking specimens are different. Shortly they should be able to identify each species specifically.

Nevertheless, most of the varieties available in reputable outlets are true to their labels. But the performance of these varieties in the wide range of local conditions is not consistently recorded. Neither is the local performance of recent imports in this country. This problem is added to by the need of most olive growers to be commercially competitive with a

'I get annoyed by environmentalists who want to pull out feral olive trees. Those who say that olive trees are noxious have rocks in their heads.'
Don Evangelista

'Birds, animals and people can live off the olive tree.'
Don Evangelista

variety that makes quality oil at a high percentage. There is therefore a bottle-neck in the redevelopment of the olive industry as a modern and viable activity, and there are long waiting lists for the delivery of pre-ferred plants. Many new growers become impatient and plant whatever trees they can lay their hands on. This means potential disaster for those who are trying to make money with their olives.

Serious growers should clearly define their purpose between oil and table olive production, their method of harvesting, and their particular microclimate before opening discussions with the nurseries. They have to be prepared to wait for the varieties that will suit their land and conditions.

But there is hope for improvement in this area. The Plant Research Centre at the Waite Campus, University of Adelaide has started the National Olive Variety Assessment Project to develop specific typing techniques in conjuction with the Feral and Colonial Plant Improvement Program at the same place, and soon there should be some good data from which olive growers can work.

chemistry

Although there is an increasing understanding of the olive's chemical processes, there remains an infinite mystery about much of what happens in this magical mythical fruit. Scientists cannot reduce it all to simple equations.

Olive oil is composed mainly of glycerol molecules, onto which are attached three fatty acid molecules in various combinations to give triacylglycerols (or triglycerides, as they are commonly called).

In nature there are many fatty acids which occur widely as essential chemicals in metabolism, but in olive oil there are only thirteen. The six in highest concentration and their chemical formulae are:

OLEIC ACID (monounsaturated)

$CH.(CH_2)_7.COOH$

$\|$

$CH. (CH_2)_7.CH_3$

LINOLEIC ACID (doubly unsaturated)

$CH_3.(CH_2)_4.CH$

$\|$

$CH.CH_2.CH$

$\|$

$CH.(CH_2)_7.COOH$

PALMITIC ACID (saturated)

$CH_3.(CH_2)_4.COOH$

PALMITOLEIC ACID (monounsaturated)

$CH_3.(CH_2)_5.CH=\!=\!=CH.(CH_2)_7.COOH$

STEARIC ACID (saturated)

$CH_3.(CH_2)_{16}.COOH$

LINOLENIC ACID (triply unsaturated)

$CH.CH_2.CH=\!=\!=CH.CH_2.CH_3$

$\|$

$CH.CH_2.CH=\!=\!=CH.(CH_2)_7.COOH$

The proportions of the fatty acids in a particular oil not only give the oil its overall style, but significantly determine its keeping qualities as a fruit juice.

The double lines between the 'Cs' represent unsaturated bonds between carbon atoms. This means that there is a possibility of chemical interaction – in this context with oxygen to cause oxidation or rancidity. So, if an oil has a lot of linolenic acid, which has three unsaturated bonds and is therefore twenty-five times more likely to oxidise than oleic acid, it will be an unstable oil that does not keep well.

Oxidation is the chemical process that causes rancidity in an oil. Once present, rancidity is irreversible. It occurs in every oil as it ages, but clearly it is better to start out with an oil low in unsaturated fatty acids, and which has high natural antioxidant levels.

The amount of oxidation that has occurred in an oil can be measured in the laboratory and given as a peroxide value – the lower the better. The resistance to oxidation, which translates into stability and shelf life, can be measured as the rancimat induction time – the longer the better. The proportions of fatty acids also have a bearing on the value of olive oil in prevention of heart vessel disease.

Most people are concerned about the colour, smell and flavour of olive oil, rather than its keeping properties (though the two go together). There are a huge number of minor components in olive oil, most of which are obscure and difficult to group. A few of the known ones are:

tocopherols

These are the vitamin E group. They have antioxidant properties, and are sometimes called free radical quenchers. Their concentration in oils varies widely from five to 300 parts per million, and in part depends on the variety. The levels are higher from an early harvest, and, unlike the levels of the polyphenols, they can increase if olives stand before crushing.

pigments

These include chlorophylls, pheophytins and carotenoids. Pigments tend to diminish as ripening proceeds, with carotene coming to dominate. They are said to be higher in centrifuged than in pressed oil.

polyphenols

This complex group of compounds exists in a wide range of concentrations from fifty to 200 parts per million, and in some oils can be as high as 1000 parts per million. They are antioxidants, and they contribute to flavour. Among them is the bitter glycoside oleouropein which decreases in concentration as ripening proceeds. There is some disagreement about the effect of centrifugal extraction on these important taste-contributing compounds.

volatile and aroma compounds

There is a huge list of these compounds in olive oil and their individual contribution to smell is unclear. Researchers around the world are involved in the sport of 'GC sniffing', the name for breaking up oil in a gas chromatograph and smelling each component. The concentrations of these minor components in an oil will depend on the olive variety, the season and cultivation practices, the timing of harvest, and the handling and extraction methods.

lipase enzymes

From the moment of picking, lipase enzymes will be at work breaking down the triacylglycerols by splitting off the fatty acid molecules which then appear in the oil as free fatty acids. These are a mixture of all the fatty acids originally present, but when this free fatty acidity is measured, just oleic acid is used in the calculation because it is the predominant one. The free fatty acidity of an oil is thus expressed in milligrams per 100 millilitres, or as a percentage as if it were all oleic acid.

free acidity

A low free acidity is desirable in an oil because it reflects a gentle production from sound fruit which was not too ripe. Free acidity is the main criterion used when grading the quality of oils. On the other hand, in the better oils the oleic acid levels in the intact oil should be high.

From the chemical point of view, there is a rationale for enlightened olive cultural practices.

best practice

Varieties that produce an oil with high levels of saturated and mono-unsaturated fatty acids will be preferred.

Varieties that produce oils with high levels of polyphenols and tocopherols will be preferred.

Early harvesting will ensure higher levels of polyphenols and tocopherols.

Prompt pressing after gentle handling will give the lipases less opportunity to raise the free acidity.

extracting olive oil

The challenge in extracting oil from the olive is to get most of it from within the cells and tissues of the olive's flesh by gentle means that do not alter the structure of the oil, do not lose the minor compounds so important to smell and taste, and do not add any undesirable taints.

The big enemies are air, heat, water, excessive mechanical forces and chemical interactions. Exposure to the air brings oxidation which makes the oil rancid. Heat speeds up the degenerative processes and drives off volatile flavours and smells. Added water washes away important minor components. Excessive mechanical forces create heat and promote degeneration. Chemical interaction with reactive metals such as copper can promote oxidation. These adverse influences promote the action of lipase enzymes which split off the fatty acids and increase the acidity. UV light also promotes oxidation and dictates methods of storage.

The computer rule of GIGO (garbage in – garbage out) applies to olive oil, and it is important that the correct variety of olive is used for a particular style of oil. The olives need to be fresh and not deteriorating from being transported and stored in humid sacks.

Traditional methods of extraction are now seldom used, although it was these methods that produced terminology that is still used today.

The most expensive olive oil on a gourmet grocery shop shelves may be Benza and Lupi 'Primuruggiu'. On the back label of these oils there is a promotional blurb followed by 'VARIETA: Oliva nostrana Taggiasca. RACCOLTA: Valle di Dolcedo e colline che la circondano. FRANTOIO: Tradizionale a macina di pietra colombina. LAVORAZIONE: Grondatura spontanea – Primuruggiu'. This information lists the variety of olives, where they were grown, that they were milled between Columbian stone, and that the oil was the first oil that came away from the paste spontaneously under the influence of gravity. This method of extraction must be the nearest thing to the ancient practice of putting olives in a sack and putting a large rock on top. The carved-out bottom rocks in the Hittite caves in central Turkey, which were used for this purpose, still exist.

After industrialisation, the animal-turned grinding wheels and hand-

In 1956 Luigi Bazzani founded the Olea Nursery. He recently moved to the Margaret River district. He has bred his own olives and he is known as one of the best suppliers in Australia.

operated screw olive presses gave way to machine-driven versions, but the underlying processes of the traditional method remained the same.

The traditional method involved milling between stone wheels and a stone baseplate to crush the flesh and stone, allowing the droplets of contained oil to be released. Some of this would come together and form globules as the milling proceeded. The resulting paste was shovelled into porous sacks, or spread between mats which were then slowly pressed to a low pressure, with the resulting oil being collected as the 'first pressed' oil. (The oil which came away at the very beginning was prized as the 'flowers'.) The paste was then returned to the mill for a second time. The oil and vegetable water would be allowed to separate spontaneously in settling tanks, and the spent paste, or pomace, would go off for industrial uses. All of this would be done at the prevailing room temperature, so the oil could accurately also be labelled 'cold pressed'.

This tedious, messy, labour-intensive and slow process yields the highest percentage of oil, and it is the first-pressed cold-pressed oil which remains as the gold standard for quality virgin olive oils. But as the inefficient traditional process was modernised the extraction process began to incorporate machines to clean, wash, crush and pre-crush the olives and kneading or mixing machines for the paste which would be spread automatically onto the mats.

The traditional method gives more oil of high quality, is a simple technology which can be maintained locally, and uses little energy other than human. But it is labour-intensive and messy, requiring a lot of effort to keep everything clean to avoid 'off' flavours.

These new machines helped speed up the extraction process, but presented a problem with the need to batch the olives and paste when loading up the mill and the press, resulting in a stop-start or saltatory process. When pump and centrifuge technology provided the opportunity to transfer the materials between machines in pipes, and large horizontal centrifuges could separate the oil and water from the solid matter, it was

possible to develop a 'continuous process' extraction plant – olives in one end and oil out the other. This process involves cleaning, (hammer) milling, mixing, separation from solids and then separation from vegetable water.

Such a challenge to tradition caused controversy, and the introduction of the early three-phase (oil, water and solids) horizontal centrifuges started a passionate debate that still continues.

The efficiency of the new process was offset by the high electrical energy use and initial capital outlay, and the need for a trained operator and expert repair and maintenance. The oil yields were lower, and occasionally an emulsion would develop, taking all the oil out with the waste water.

Paradoxically there is less control over the extraction process when advanced technology is used, and this shows up when confronted with 'difficult' olives. But more important, from the point of view of quality, is the transient rise in temperature in the hammer mill and centrifuge, and the leaching effect of the added water (especially if hot).

The polyphenol concentrations were reduced and the flavours were altered in the new method. But such was the convenience of the continuous process, that in true Procrustean fashion, 'harsh' was removed from the list of defects, and most people got used to the reduction in flavour. Some people even find it possible to continue calling oil 'cold pressed' when the oil was extracted by a centrifuge using heated water.

Fortunately, with the advent of the new generation of two-phase decanters in which no water is added, the difference is being reduced. In the meantime, those who want top-quality oil from a three-phase decanter should monitor the temperature of the added water and keep it below 28°C. When engineers are able to get the temperatures down in the centrifuges, the only other concern will be the milling.

Those inclined to stick with pressing – usually the smaller or independent grower – have abandoned the classical method and taken up a single pressing method. Some use super presses with very high pressures, but a typical small press rises through 100 times normal atmospheric pressure to 400 times normal atmospheric pressure over an hour. Mechanised winnowing, washing and conveyer belts speed up the arrival at the hammer mill. The paste is mixed in the chamber below the mill for about twenty minutes before being spread onto mats semi-automatically and transferred as a stack to be pressed. After pressing, the mats have to be cleaned of the spent pomace and used again. Keeping the mats clean and free from taints is a challenge. The mixed oil and vegetable water is usually left to separate by itself and the water decanted from the top, or it can be separated in a centrifuge.

In larger commercial mills the oil is filtered just after pressing. Otherwise it is done after about three months.

Although centrifugal extraction occupies the centre stage of big industry, there are a number of quite different methods lurking in the wings. 'Percolation' (selective filtration) relies on the surface tension differential between oil and water. In this method a metal comb or similar is passed through the paste and the oil collects on the prongs. This principle has been in use since 1911, with the modern version being known as the SINOLEA system, which has some huge models. This simple process leaves behind a considerable amount of oil, so combinations with a mopping-up centrifuge are being tried. Early reports show that this combination achieves much the same result as the single pressing system.

The environmental impact of the new, no-added water, two-phase centrifuge is less than with the three-phase machine but with a number of mills it will be necessary and profitable to set up plants for industrial oil extraction of the spent pomace. There will consequently be regional development challenges in the future as a result of the present planting spree.

While wine tasting is a structured and well-known practice, two differences stand out when it comes to official olive oil tasting. The first is that in an official oil tasting, the appearance of the oil is not supposed to count, and only taste, smell and common chemical stimuli are considered to contribute. To this end, blue glass containers are used to hide the oil. Most people respond to the appearance of an oil, but they also respond to the 'feel' of the oil, which is not scored.

The second difference is that, unlike wine, oil is never better than in the year of its extraction, though some green or wild olives or both produce an initially feisty oil that mellows in six months or so. Tasting freshly pressed oil at a mill in Tuscany can be a fiery experience as the cough-inducing after-taste (which is known as 'pungency') seizes the back of your throat.

To make the most of an olive oil tasting you need to understand how virgin olive oils are classified and to keep in mind the purpose of a particular tasting – whether it is for trade classification under the International Olive Oil Council's regulations, for competition, or just for fun. The council's accredited tasting panels use just a few criteria to classify oils for marketing purposes, and these are aimed at weeding out oils made badly – the 'rotten apple' approach to quality assurance. In competition tasting, there are different interpretations of the oil's attributes, with the pursuit of excellence as the primary focus. This focus should be more applicable to much of the quality oil now being made in Australia. The International Movement for Olive Oil Culture in Florence and Jos Mojet have each developed their own methods for judging oils.

The International Olive Oil Council's definition of virgin olive oils has three components. Firstly, the oils must be extracted from sound olive fruit by only the simple mechanical processes of milling, pressing and centrifuging. No chemical or excessive heat extraction is allowed, although the actual temperature is not specified and this can be an important determinant of quality.

Secondly, the oils must meet a number of chemical tests aimed at detecting breakdown products or adulteration. The latter employ sophisticated chromatography in an attempt to maintain the distinction between virgin olive oil and the rapidly changing manipulated seed oils that can now be made to look quite similar. The traditional test for breakdown is the measurement of free fatty acid, and this is still used as a key criterion for dividing virgin oils into the categories extra virgin (acidity less than 1 per cent), virgin (less than 2 per cent), ordinary virgin (less than 3.3 per cent), and lampante virgin (more than 3.3 per cent) which is not suitable for consumption without refining.

Thirdly, the oil must pass an accredited tasting panel's organoleptic, or sensory, assessment, a method of evaluation that was developed by the council in 1994. This process adds a subjective component to the definition of oils, and it remains to be seen how just how Europe will implement such a methodology in the market place.

Until November 1996, tasters sought just six defects for the sensory assessment. This was done with much loud slurping and sucking which was politely named 'aspiration', followed by genteel expectoration. The defects and their causes were defined in this way.

from olives stored in piles that had undergone fermentation	• FUSTY
from fungi and yeasts in olives stored in humid conditions	• MUSTY
from prolonged contact with sediment in storage containers	• MUDDY SEDIMENT
from the formation of excessive amounts of acetic acid, ethyl acetate and ethanol	• WINEY SOUR ACID
from contact with metals during processing	• METALLIC
from oxidation (the worst defect).	• RANCID

If any of these defects were perceived in sufficient intensity by the panel, the oil was relegated to the lampante classification.

On 20 November 1996, the goal posts were moved. Other defects were to be taken into account if they were perceived by over half of the tasting panel. These were:

from excessive or prolonged heating of the paste	• HEATED OR BURNT
from olives that had dried out	• HAY-WOOD
a thick pasty sensation	• ROUGH
from residual petroleum grease on machinery	• GREASY
from prolonged contact with vegetable water in extraction	• VEGETABLE WATER
from salted olives	• BRINE
from oil pressed on new esparto mats	• ESPARATO
from soiled unwashed olives	• EARTHY
from olives attacked by the olive fly	• GRUBBY
from the oil being hermetically sealed in tin containers for a long time.	• CUCUMBER

The tasters then rated the oil's good qualities.

FRESH OLIVE FRUITNESS • The characteristic smell and then taste of fresh olives which give either ripe or green fruitiness.

BITTERNESS • transient on the middle palate due to some greenness

PUNGENCY • a biting sensation in the whole mouth, and later the throat – characteristic of olives picked early in the season.

These attributes had to be present in moderation and balance. The panel supervisor manipulates the score cards and comes up with a median score for attributes and defects, which, in conjunction with acidity, are used to grade the virgin oil as:

EXTRA VIRGIN • no defects, with fruitiness, and an acidity less than 1 per cent

VIRGIN • defects scoring zero to 2.5, with fruitiness, and an acidity 1 to 2 per cent

ORDINARY VIRGIN • defects from 2.5 to 6 if fruity, or less than 2.5 if not fruity, and an acidity from 2 to 3.3 per cent

LAMPANTE • a defect score greater than 6, and/or an acidity above 3.3 per cent.

As with wine tasting, the method of oil tasting is individual, but usually you warm the glass in cupped hands and take a brief sniff to get an immediate impression. Then you take a deeper smell to confirm, expand or change your mind about your first impression. You then take a teaspoonful of oil, roll it around in your mouth, and suck air in through your clenched teeth. Then you swallow it or spit it out, having noted the taste on the initial and middle palates. The taste on the after palate is sometimes quite delayed.

The bland sweet oils that many Australians prefer are regarded as featureless by the cognoscenti who incline to the robust assertive oils typical of northern Italy, which have dominated those from the south, where sweet golden oil from ripe fruit allowed to fall on the ground is favoured. Many of the recent varietal pressings that have emerged from the Australian groves, and especially from feral olives, have been full of flavour with some bitterness and pungency.

Although only nine criteria are used in the official olive oil tastings, here are some other terms used for informal tastings:

- **ALMOND** the fresh almond or dried almond aftertaste which is associated with sweet oils of flat smell, and can be confused with rancidity
- **APPLE** the taste of apples
- **FLAT, SMOOTH OR WEAK** from loss of or lack of aromatic compounds (see sweet)
- **GRASS** a smell of newly mown grass green leaves (bitter) from excessively green olives or leaves and twigs included in the crushing
- **OLD** seemingly a polite way of saying 'rancid'
- **POMACE** of oils extracted from the residue after pressing
- **PRESSING MAT** from unclean mats which are fermenting
- **SOAPY** a soapy feeling in the mouth
- **SWEET** from weak bitter, astringent and pungent attributes.

There are, of course, many other terms used by people as they try to describe their perceptions of an olive oil. Not everyone has the same sensory capacity or has been trained at the same level. It usually takes a novice five or six sessions before they can select particular tastes and smells.

An alternative to the council's method is the one devised by the Movement for the Olive Oil Culture. In 1994, this organisation listed six merits and seven defects of olive oils. The merits must be prefixed by a clean taste and a total absence of defects.

The merits are:

FRESHNESS • the sensation of freshly squeezed fruit with a significant aroma

SPICINESS • present for some months after crushing. This after-taste takes a while to disappear after swallowing.

HARMONY • when the fragrance, taste and tactile sensation are in perfect equilibrium

FRUITINESS • the total of the aromas that remain intense and stable for at least a year after crushing

GENTLENESS • the light combination of flavour and fragrance, typical of certain production zones and varieties

BITTERNESS • the bitter sensation that is felt on the back palate – this can be present in an oil for some months after crushing. When it persists for some minutes after swallowing, it is considered a defect.

The defects are:

RANCIDITY • the unpleasant sensation of over-ripe melons or pumpkins resulting from the ageing of an oil caused by light, heat or oxidation

MOULDINESS • the dank taste which inhibits salivation and is a result of poor conservation of the olives before milling

SCALDING • the taste of boiled or overcooked pulses. This also results from poor conservation of the olives before milling, as well as elevated temperature during extraction.

VINEGARY • the astringent taste of vinegar which comes from the fermentation of olives that are put in piles while waiting to be crushed

the unclean taste that results from prolonged contact between the oil
  and the residue of the olives during extraction
the soapy tactile sensation from olives that have been attacked by the
  olive fly
the absence of harmony and general cleanliness resulting from the
  crushing of olives in different states of maturity and from
  inadequate conservation.

- SEDIMENT
- FATTINESS
- COARSENESS

There are difficulties, however, with the two processes of judging olive oils. Some people have the ability to detect and identify subtle flavours and smells, and to reach a broad consensus on the attributes or defects of the oil, but both methods rely on objectifying an essentially subjective experience.

So, what is a good olive oil? When asked this perennial question, Alicia Rios Ivars, the famous Spanish writer and gastronome, said that each oil is like a landscape and, like landscapes, they will be more or less pleasing to different people, and to the same person at different times. Nevertheless, there is consensus that the defects outlined in the council's method should be avoided by those who want their oil to be accepted on the quality market. In the end, of course, fashion will continue to dictate the acceptable flavour of the times.

Both the International Olive Oil Council and the Australian Olive Oil Association (importers and wholesalers) have guidelines for labelling on such questions as volume, batch number, and format. The arguments over how the country of origin is to be displayed, and the debate about the final regulations for 'Product of Australia' and 'Made in Australia' indicate how easy it is in the process to lose sight of the original purpose.

International and national standards and gradings for olive oil do exist. The consumer has the right to accuracy on labels so that they can make an informed choice. Of seven Australian extra virgin olive oils recently tested, for example, five were up to standard, one was just outside it, and only one needed to be classified as lampante. As the monitoring system is refined, this should improve.

The public is generally ill informed about olive oil gradings and quality. But public education is growing. The Australian Olive Association, which includes olive growers and oil producers, is considering its policy on labelling. It seems likely that it will recommend that an informative label should also be provided. This label might include: olive variety, place of growth, harvesting details, extraction method and date, results of any analysis (at least the acidity), and results of any sensory assessment. Such labelling should educate and inform the buyer.

acknowledgements

The authors and publisher wish to thank the following chefs and publishers for permission to reprint their recipes.

Olive bread; grape and olive bread; olive foccacia; ajo blanco; fetta and olives; marinated olives; Stephanie Alexander, *The Cook's Companion*, Viking, 1996.

Mayonnaise; anchovy and olive butter; chicken pieces roasted with olives, preserved lemon and fennel; skate with capers and olives; oxtail with orange, olives and walnuts; Maggie Beer, *Maggie's Orchard*, Viking, 1997.

Green olive gnocchi with green olive sauce; Maggie Beer, *Maggie's Farm*, Allen & Unwin, 1993.

Roasted garlic aïoli; grilled rare tuna steak with fennel, green garlic and roasted aïoli; Chris Manfield, *Paramount Cooking*, Viking, 1996.

authors' note

karen reichelt and michael burr

We would like to thank Stephanie Johnston and Michael Bollen of Wakefield Press for their encouragement and support. Our thanks also go to our editor, Jane Arms, and to Fiona Oates who did early work on the manuscript.

Thanks to the following olive growers, producers and chefs for giving so generously of their time in sharing their experiences and recipes with Karen Reichelt:

Napoleon Niarchos, Joe Grilli, Emmanuel Giakoumis, Don Evangelista, Mark Lloyd, Jane Ferrari, Luigi Bazzani, Geoff and Lynette Winfield. Ann Oliver, Chris Manfield, Cath Kerry, Rosa Matto, Stephanie Alexander, Stefano Manfredi, Connie Rotolo, Lew Kathreptis, Zeffie Kathreptis, Irene Cashman, Seb Bosh, Ian Parmenter, Maggie Beer and Russell Jeavons.

We would also like to thank Eduardo Gonzale of the Embassy of Spain, Philippa Goodrich and Louise Fewtrell of the International Olive Oil Council, Barbara Santich, Simon Johnson, John Newton and John Newton Senior for their advice and assistance.

The *Adelaide Observer*, 19 August 1843, 22 February 1862, 20 July 1870.

The *Age*, 26 November 1988, 20 November 1990, 18 February 1992,
    15 October 1996.

ALLEN, W.J., 1900, Agricultural Gazette of New South Wales.

The *Australasian* (Melbourne), 10 August 1901, 4 July 1908.

'An Australian Colony: the government handbook of Victoria', 1898, Melbourne,
    Government Printer.

The *Australian Town and Country Journal*, Sydney, 11 June 1898.

BAROSSA VALLEY OLIVE PLANTATIONS LTD, 1960, *Gold from the Barossa*.

BERNAYS, Lewis Adolphus, 1883, Cultural Industries for Queensland: Papers on the
    cultivation of useful plants suited to the climate of Queensland; Their value as
    food, in the arts, and in medicine: and methods of obtaining their products, Brisbane,
    Government Printer.

BLYTH-KLEIN, A. 1983, *The Feast of the Olive*, Berkeley, California, Aris Books.

Brisbane *Courier*, 24 November 1875.

BROCK, K. Alleyne, 1956, *Growing Olives for Profit*.

BURR, Michael, 1997, *Australian Olives: A guide for Growers and Producers of
    Virgin Oils*.

BUSBY, James, 1834, Journal of a recent visit to the principal vineyards of Spain
    and France.

The *Chronicle*, Toowoomba, 25 January 1983.

DAVENPORT, Sir Samuel, nd, *Cultivation of the Olive*.

DAVENPORT, Sir Samuel, 1864, *Some New Industries for South Australia*.

de AMEZUA, Clara and ARENILLAS, Engeles and CAPEL, Jose Carlos, 1988, *From Spain with Olive Oil*, Barcelona, Asoliva.

DOLAMORE, Anne, 1994, *A Buyer's Guide to Olive Oil*, London, Grub Street.

DOLAMORE, Anne, 1988, *The Essential Olive Oil Companion*, Sun, Australia.

GRIMAL, Pierre, 1965, *Larouse World Mythology*, Secaucus, New Jersey, Chartwell Books.

HARTMANN, Hudson, nd, 'Olive growing in Australia', in *Journal of Economic Botany*, University of California.

The *Herald* (City edition), 21 May 1980.

The *Herald*, 19 March 1981.

HILL, Ernestine, 1937, *Water into Gold*, Melbourne, Robertson & Mullens.

The *Leader*, 7 June 1890, 23 April 1904.

International Olive Oil Council, 1996, *Mediterranean Cooking with Olive Oil*, Madrid.

McGEE, Harold, 1990, *The Curious Cook*, San Francisco, North Point Press.

McGEE, Harold, 1984, *On Food and Cooking*, New York, Scribner.

MAIDEN, J.H., 1917, 'The olive: Its introduction to Australia', in the *Agricultural Gazette of New South Wales*, 3 December 1917.

MANFREDI, Stefano, paper delivered at International Olive Oil Conference.

MANFREDI, Stefano, in the *Financial Review*, 1 September 1995, 7 June 1996.

MARCH, Lourdes and RIOS, Alicia, 1988, 'Olives – an ancestral tradition faces the future', in *Food Conservation: Ethnological Studies*, London, Prospect Books.

INTERNATIONAL OLIVE OIL COUNCIL, nd, *The Olive Tree, The Oil, The Olive*, Madrid.

PERKINS, A.J., 1917, 'On the scope in South Australia for extension of olive groves', *Bulletin 11*, South Australia, Department of Agriculture.

RIOS, Alicia, 1986, 'Olive Oil, Balsamic Medium', in *The Cooking Medium, Proceedings of the Oxford Symposium on Food and Cooking*, London, Prospect Books.

Robinvale ... the first fifty years, Back-to-Robinvale for the 50th anniversary committee, Robinvale, 1975.

SALIER, Cecil W., *Journal of the Royal Australian Historical Society*, Vol 17, Part 1 and Part 2.

SHEPHERD, T.W., 1851, *Catalogue of plants cultivated at the Darling Nursery*.

SLUGA, Glenda, 1988, *Bonegilla: A place of no hope*, Melbourne University, History Department.

The *South Australian Register*, 20 June, 20 July 1870, 17 June 1875, 1 January 1876.

Sunday Times, nd, Perth.

'Elixir of youth in olive oil', in the *Australian*, 7 April 1997.

VISSER, Margaret, 1986, *Much Depends on Dinner*, New York, Grove Press.